HELP FOR
BEDWETTING

Dr Roger Morgan has an initial degree in education, and a PhD for his work on the treatment of bedwetting. After working as Research Fellow at the Child Treatment Research Unit in Birmingham, he was appointed head of research at Kent Social Services Department, then Assistant Director of Social Services for Cambridgeshire. He is now Deputy Director and Chief Inspector of Social Services for Oxfordshire. In addition to his work to help children and adults with the problem of bedwetting, he invented the widely used Paired Reading method for parents to help their children read.

Roger Morgan has run bedwetting treatment clinics for over 20 years, lectures widely on bedwetting and its treatment, and has published numerous research papers on the subject. He currently directs the Enuresis Treatment Service, a registered charity running both an Oxford based clinic, and 'Treatline', a nationally available 'open clinic' treating both children and adults through regular telephone and postal contact.

His other books are *Behavioural Treatments for Children* and *Helping Children Read*. Roger Morgan is married, with two daughters.

Help for the Bedwetting Child

*A guide to the problem
of bedwetting and its treatment
for parents and professionals*

ROGER MORGAN, BA, PhD
Illustrated by Kevin Maddison

CEDAR

TO MY FAMILY

A Mandarin Paperback
HELP FOR THE BEDWETTING CHILD

First published in Great Britain 1988
by Methuen Children's Books
This revised edition published 1992 by Cedar
an imprint of Mandarin Paperbacks
Michelin House, 81 Fulham Road, London SW3 6RB

Mandarin is an imprint of the Octopus Publishing Group,
a division of Reed International Books Limited

Text copyright © Dr Roger Morgan 1988, 1991
Illustrations copyright © Kevin Maddison 1988

A CIP catalogue record for this title
is available from the British Library
ISBN 0 7493 1079 0

Printed and bound in Great Britain
by Cox & Wyman Ltd, Reading, Berks

CONTENTS

Acknowledgements

The opinions in this book are my own, but I wish to express my gratitude to those researchers and therapists on whose research I have drawn, from whose experience I have learned, and with whom I have worked. In particular, I am indebted to my colleagues at special incontinence clinics: to Dr Gordon Young at Barnet, who first taught me how to treat bedwetting; to Dr Keith Turner, Professor Derek Jehu and Professor Martin Herbert when we were together at Leicester and Birmingham; to Dr Don Brooksbank and Dr Joan Hay at Chatham; to Dr Gwen Gresham in Cambridge; and to Dr Aidan Macfarlane in Oxford.

I am also indebted to the many parents and children who have worked so hard on so many courses of treatment, and who have always been so willing to take part in the development of techniques and the evaluation of their treatment at research clinics.

Finally, I am grateful to my colleagues at Octopus Books for their helpful support, and to Helen, Ruth and Jennifer for, as always, being so tolerant of my writing activities.

RM

PREFACE

I have written this book to give both parents and professionals (such as GP's, health visitors, school nurses, continence advisers social workers and foster parents) a handbook of information which contains practical tips about bedwetting and its treatment, together with practical information about the related problems of daytime wetting and soiling. I have drawn on my own experience over years of treating a large number of children and young people suffering from the problem. I also hope that some of the older children and young people will themselves find the book readable and helpful.

I wrote the first edition to be published in 1981 for the Disabled Living Foundation. The book was well received, but eventually went both out of print and out of date. This was followed by a second edition, and now the third, revised and brought up to date with latest equipment and research findings. I hope that the result is a book especially tuned to the needs of families who wish to seek guidance privately from a handbook rather than, or as well as, through professional channels. The book also includes guidance for professionals setting up and running treatment clinics.

I became interested in the study and treatment of bedwetting in children as a newly-fledged research worker in 1970, and have been involved ever since because of three factors. Firstly, there is the extreme personal importance of bedwetting to the child and his or her family. Secondly, the knowledge that something *can* be done, successfully, to help the majority of children to overcome their bedwetting problem – even if the commonly given assurance is that it is 'nothing to worry about' and that 'he (or she) will probably grow out of it eventually'. Thirdly – and perhaps most importantly – there is the fact that many, many children have tried various routines and treatments with disappointing results; this is mainly because knowledge of the techniques and details of their practical use is nowhere nearly available enough to either parents or professionals. It is also sad (and all too common at the special clinics in which I have worked) to meet a boy or girl who has used the enuresis alarm – a quite effective but difficult treatment described in this book – with disappointing results because they have fallen into some of the basic pitfalls of the technique, and the initial explanation and subsequent supervision failed to prevent this.

These three factors led to this book being written. I hope that it will help to explain what is behind both bedwetting and the skills of staying clean and dry, assist in deciding whether and when to seek professional advice, give some ideas for 'self-help' at home, and be a source of useful information when using complex treatment procedures.

A number of children who wet the bed have problems with daytime wetting, or with their bowel control. I have therefore discussed both these problems briefly and suggested some basic ways of dealing with them. There is also a section on helping the child or young person with a mental handicap who suffers from bladder or bowel control problems.

Throughout the book, I have tried to stress two main themes. Firstly, the way bladder control problems can be countered by nothing more mysterious than carefully planned *learning*. Secondly, the importance of *recording* on a simple chart the effects of whatever helping technique is tried. Too many treatment efforts are carried out without recording any progress that is made – yet only by consistently recording progress can treatment techniques be 'fine tuned' to increase effectiveness.

Roger Morgan,
Oxford, October 1991

ONE

INTRODUCTION

There can be few social and physical problems more devastating to one's sense of personal dignity than the inability to exercise full control over bladder or bowel. Those who have not experienced such problems themselves cannot fully imagine the feelings of a child who cannot go to sleep at night without the fear that his or her body will let them down while they are asleep and out of control, so that they awake in a urine-soaked bed; or those of the child who, despite desperate efforts to prevent it, soils his or her underclothes with faeces and has to suffer not only personal disgrace and failure, but also the taunts of other children. In the face of such problems, some children not surprisingly react with signs of stress and disturbance as well, while others can only survive by adopting a blasé and devil-may-care attitude. Even in the latter case, it is worth bearing in mind that few children would wet the bed, wet their pants or soil themselves if they could help it.

The consequences of wetting or soiling are very severe for the child concerned. The typical bedwetting child tries to keep his or her problem a secret from all but the closest of relatives or friends, and realises all too clearly the limitations that bedwetting brings when he does not dare to go to stay with friends, go on school holidays, or to Scout or Guide camps. Bedwetting is a problem for many teenagers and young people as well as children, and the young people concerned realise acutely the restriction bedwetting places upon jobs which require residential training or residential work, such as nursing, college study or joining the forces, or simply living away from home. For someone with daytime

I

wetting or soiling, the problem is there for all to see. Few children wish to sit next to, or make friends with, a child who smells of urine or faeces. The parents of a child or young person with incontinence problems owe it to their son or daughter to do their best to understand the problem and to help to overcome it by the best means available.

For a parent, the fact that their child wets the bed or soils can prove severely testing. The problem brings with it a heavy and unpleasant washload, often day in, day out. This is particularly difficult if washing facilities are limited, living conditions are crowded, or if buying enough clothing and bedclothing is a problem. Added to this, relatives and other parents are often critical. Having a child who wets or soils can very easily be taken as a sign of some sort of failure in the parent. It is widely recognised that wetting and soiling are amongst the most difficult problems that parents may face with their children. The situation is made worse by the fact that most parents are unsure whether a wet or soiled older child can, or cannot 'help it'; whether they should sympathise, punish or ignore the problem, and why their particular child or children should seem to be so behind in this respect. It is extremely difficult to deal consistently and rationally with a problem that can be so persistent, off-putting and frustrating to all concerned.

It is probably because it *is* so basic a problem that bedwetting has become the focus of a wealth of folk lore, and most parents and children involved are likely to come across a wide variety of advice, much of it conflicting and confusing. Opinions differ widely amongst doctors, child psychologists, health visitors, and the other professionals involved. It is, however, vital to the success of management and treatment of the problem that parents should have information available on the principles and procedures involved. Without such information, it can become difficult, if not impossible, to apply and adapt procedures to one's own child and household, and to cope with unexpected setbacks and difficulties. It is also difficult to know exactly what to expect, and how soon to start, when using a particular technique to cope with or to treat the problem. Quite apart from their parents, the children who have the wetting or soiling problem feel far happier if both the problem and its treatment are explained to them in terms that they can understand – and parents need adequate information before they can pass it on to their children.

The next chapter of this book provides basic information about the nature and development of both bladder and bowel control, and about the way the relevant parts of the body work. The following chapters give detailed information about the problem of bedwetting, and describe some of the most common management procedures that may be used by parents, as well as the treatments most likely to be advised by doctors, health visitors, or others who may be consulted professionally. The pros and cons of major alternative approaches are outlined, and some common misconceptions discussed. Practical guidance is given on the very effective, but not always easy, use of the enuresis alarm to treat bedwetting, followed by brief chapters on the treatment of daytime wetting and soiling. There has been a considerable amount of research into children's bladder and bowel control problems and their treatment, and this book has been written with such research firmly in mind.

The use of the enuresis alarm as a treatment for bedwetting (or enuresis) is dealt with in some detail in this book, to give sufficient guidance to enable both parents and their professional advisers to use this treatment successfully with the majority of bedwetting children and young people. Alarms can be obtained through the National Health Service, but they can also be purchased privately direct from the manufacturers for use at home.

It is intended that the information given should help parents and children to consider and discuss their particular wetting or soiling problem, and to decide whether and when to seek professional advice. It is also intended to provide background information to help parents, children and young people when they are discussing the problems and alternative courses of action with the doctor or any other person they consult, and to build upon the limited amount of information which can be given during a brief professional consultation. The information given may suggest a solution to less severe wetting or soiling problems, but even where professional help is needed, that help is likely to be more effectively used, and to be less frightening to a child, if the parents and child are reasonably well informed about the basic facts. For most people, discussing something as personal and distressing as wetting or soiling can be painfully embarrassing, and it is hoped that this book will answer some questions so that they do not have to be asked of anyone else. While it is aimed primarily at parents, the older boy or girl with a wetting or soiling problem may find that reading the book in private is preferable to trying to talk about the problem with someone else – whether parent, doctor or other professional. The book should in addition prove of use to the professional who, while not a specialist in problems of incontinence, is called upon to advise parents and children about wetting and soiling.

One warning must be given: no book can provide a parent with the whole picture or deal with the special needs of every individual child, and while this book contains the basic information it is not a substitute for the specialised knowledge and practical skills of the doctor. While parents and others should find the information useful when giving help to a child with a wetting or soiling problem, a doctor should always be consulted when a definite problem exists. There *may* be a specific issue (perhaps an infection or a particular physical problem) that needs looking into, and most forms of treatment need experienced professional guidance as well as the kind of basic explanation that can be given in a book such as this.

TWO

BLADDER AND BOWEL CONTROL – WHAT DO THEY MEAN?

The structure and working of the bladder

The bladder is the reservoir that holds the urine made by the kidneys until it is emptied out of the body into the toilet or elsewhere. It is an expanding bag with walls of thin muscle (called the 'detrusor' muscle). This muscle relaxes to allow the bag to grow larger as it fills up with urine, and the same muscle contracts to squeeze the urine out when visiting the toilet. It is the muscle walls of the bladder beginning to contract and squeeze on the urine inside that gives a person the feeling of wanting to empty his or her bladder.

The bladder is not like a tank which just fills up until it overflows to result in a wet bed or wet pants, nor is it like a balloon which stretches as it fills up until it can stretch no more and so must be emptied. It works much harder than that, and (fortunately) can be controlled more easily. Because it is a bag made out of muscle, the bladder can make itself larger by relaxing (and stretching to let more urine in), or smaller by contracting (and squeezing the urine out). While it is filling with urine from the kidneys, the bladder's muscle walls gradually relax and stretch so that the bladder becomes steadily larger to contain more urine, without the pressure inside rising very much at all. When it fills up to its usual maximum level, it stops relaxing and instead begins to squeeze on the urine inside with waves of muscle contractions. You feel this as the urge to go to the toilet to empty your bladder. If the toilet is not visited for some time after this, the contractions become stronger, and the need to empty the bladder is therefore felt more urgently. When the toilet is reached, or when wetting happens, the contractions become strong enough to empty the urine out of the bladder.

Each person's bladder has its own usual maximum capacity (known as the 'functional bladder capacity'), some being very full at this point, but others containing very little urine indeed. This level is not the point at which the bladder is literally full to bursting, but rather the level at which a particular person's bladder is used to starting its contractions, and so needs to be emptied. Most importantly this usual maximum level of most people's bladders can be altered by a change in habits, as will be described in Chapter Eight. Simply drinking less, however, does not help a child with a wetting problem, since it is one of the ways of encouraging the bladder to adjust itself to a *lower* maximum level of filling than before.

Figure 1 shows the basic structure of the bladder and its inlets and outlet. The urine flows from the two kidneys to the bladder along the two tubes known as ureters, which join the bladder itself at an angle so that when the bladder is very full, or is contracting, the ends of the ureters are squeezed shut like valves to prevent urine from being pushed back up to the kidneys. When the bladder empties, the urine flows out through the tube known as the urethra, which opens on the outside of the body as the front passage between the legs in girls and at the end of the penis in boys.

As can be seen from **Figure 1**, the bladder has a rather important design problem for a container of liquid – its opening points downwards! Because of this, we all rely on the outlet of our bladders being kept tightly shut in order to keep the urine inside between visits to the toilet. The muscles that keep the outlet tube from the bladder (the urethra) firmly shut are the muscles of the 'pelvic floor'. These are like a thick sheet which the urethra passes through just underneath the base of the bladder, and when they are tensed (as they usually are), they push the bladder outlet up and safely closed.

To help understand how the pelvic floor muscles keep urine in, try filling a milk bottle with water and then hold

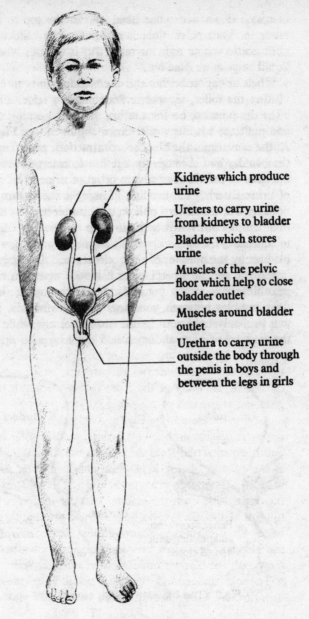

Kidneys which produce urine

Ureters to carry urine from kidneys to bladder

Bladder which stores urine

Muscles of the pelvic floor which help to close bladder outlet

Muscles around bladder outlet

Urethra to carry urine outside the body through the penis in boys and between the legs in girls

Fig.1   The urinary system

it upside down with your hand against the top to keep the water in. Your pelvic floor is rather like the hand under the milk bottle – how tight or relaxed it is decides whether the liquid stays in or runs out.

When urination begins and the bladder starts to empty on visiting the toilet, the pelvic floor muscles relax. This takes away the pressure on the urethra that was keeping it closed, and pulls the bladder outlet down and open (see **Figure 2b**). At the same time, the bladder's contractions push urine out of the bladder and through the urethra to emerge at the end of the tube as the familiar stream or jet of urine. The sensation of urine entering the urethra encourages the stream to keep flowing. The downward pull on the bladder itself as the pelvic floor drops downwards helps to keep the bladder contracting to squeeze urine out, and usually a general 'push' down on the bladder by the muscles of the abdomen and diaphragm above it helps to get the stream started. Notice what you are doing next time you empty your bladder in the toilet; the pelvic floor muscles between your legs pull downwards, and you will probably hold your breath for a moment while you use the muscles of your abdomen and diaphragm to push down

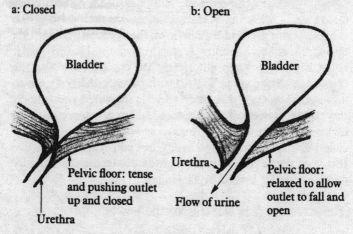

a: Closed   b: Open

Bladder   Bladder

Urethra

Pelvic floor: tense and pushing outlet up and closed

Flow of urine

Pelvic floor: relaxed to allow outlet to fall and open

Urethra

Fig.2   The bladder outlet, closed and open

8

onto the bladder to start things happening. You will probably notice the muscles of your abdomen relaxing again just before you finish emptying your bladder. People who have had an operation on the abdomen often find for a while afterwards that it is difficult to start the stream of urine going, because it will not be helped as much as usual by the abdomen and diaphragm muscles pushing down. Things return to normal when everything is healed again.

We cannot control the working of our bladders by conscious effort. Like the muscles of the heart or stomach, the bladder muscle is one of the 'automatic' muscles of the body. The muscles we use to control urination are the 'voluntary' muscles of the pelvic floor, abdomen and diaphragm, which we use to persuade the bladder to do what we want it to do, by pulling and pushing upon it. As we also use these muscles in different ways for many other things, like coughing, sneezing or laughing, their use in bladder control is complicated. It is perhaps more surprising that so many of us achieve bladder control, than that some have problems with it!

On those occasions when we stop urination in mid-stream, this is achieved by raising and tightening the pelvic floor muscles to close off the bladder outlet, squeezing the urethra closed again while the bladder contractions die down. Urine can leak out of the bladder and down the urethra to the outside during coughing, sneezing or laughing if the bladder outlet is not kept fully watertight against the extra pressure on the bladder at these times. The relevant parts of the body are so arranged, however, that when there is increased pressure on the bladder for one of these reasons, there is automatically an increased pressure on the urethra as well to help it to keep closed against accidental leakage. When you next cough, notice that your pelvic floor muscles tighten up during the pressure on your bladder caused by the cough.

The structure and working of the bowel

The structure of the lower part of the bowel is illustrated in

Figure 3. After passing through the stomach, the food being digested is pushed through the tubes of the small intestine and then the large intestine by the ripple-like waves of contractions in the muscular walls of the intestine; this process is known as 'peristalsis'. In its final sections, the large intestine (or colon) runs across the upper front part of the abdomen and then down the left-hand front side of the abdomen towards the rectum.

Unlike the colon, with its waves of peristalsis to push its contents along the tube, the rectum is usually empty, with its walls closed together to form a rather 'collapsed' tube. It is filled at intervals, rather than continuously, with the waste material (faeces) from the digestive process. When a quantity of faeces passes into the rectum, the tube stretches to store the material until the toilet is visited and the faeces emptied out.

Normally, the filling and emptying of the rectum takes place according to a more or less regular routine. This routine can be helped or changed quite markedly by the habits formed in visiting the toilet. The ability of the walls of the rectum to stretch is important to bowel control – by stretching from an empty state, quite large quantities of faeces can be stored in the rectum for short periods of time until it is convenient to empty it. It is this stretching of the walls of the rectum that gives the feeling of fullness and the urge to visit the toilet.

When the bowel is emptied (defaecation), faeces leave the rectum and pass outside the body through the ring of muscle of the anus. The anus can be controlled voluntarily, and is opened at the start of defaecation, together with a more general relaxation downwards of the pelvic floor muscles. The stretched rectum naturally tends to contract to push the faeces out and so collapse to its normally closed-up state. At the same time, one uses the diaphragm and abdominal muscles to push down on the rectum to help expel the faeces. After defaecation, the anus is closed and the rectum closes in once more.

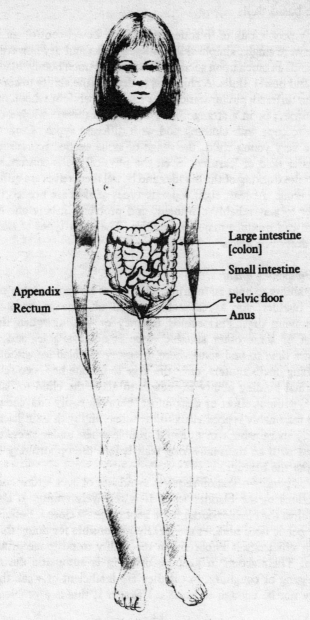

Large intestine
[colon]

Small intestine

Appendix

Rectum

Pelvic floor

Anus

Fig.3 The lower bowel

The basic skills

Many people talk of 'bladder control' or 'bowel control' as if they were single, simple skills. Staying clean and dry however depends as much upon social skills as it does upon bodily 'bladder and bowel' skills. A child has to develop the ability to cope under different circumstances (for example, while at school, on a journey, or in a strange place) as well as the knowledge of how to cope with clothing and with different types of toilet. To a very young child, the range of skills needed represents a major field of learning. Even the physical skills concerned with the working of the bladder and bowel themselves are quite numerous. At least eight separate types of skill are needed in order to stay reliably continent, and problems in any one of them can produce major difficulties. The eight types of skill are described below:

1. *Postponing urination*
The ability to hold on to urine, and thus to postpone emptying the bladder, for a reasonable period of time is essential to staying dry. This avoids urgency or wetting when the toilet or some other suitable place is not available, and it allows time to find somewhere to empty the bladder without rushing or discomfort, once the urge to urinate has been felt. Normal holding ability is enough to allow the child to 'last out', without effort or discomfort, between easily convenient and reasonably spaced visits to the toilet, and with a sufficient safety margin built in to avoid trouble when under stress or faced with an unusually long wait before the opportunity to empty the bladder.

Postponing urination requires avoidance of over-strong contractions of the bladder when it is relatively empty. It also requires the bladder outlet to be kept properly closed. Because the pelvic floor muscles are largely responsible for doing this, their efficiency is important in the ability to postpone urination. Their action in keeping urine in is automatic during sneezing or coughing, but if they are inefficient or weak this may not be enough to avoid a leakage. If this is a problem, their efficiency can often be improved by procedures such as those described in Chapter Seven. These largely automatic body functions are remarkably sensitive to change by outside influences. It is for instance common for holding ability to be reduced considerably at times of anxiety (such as examinations), when the need to visit the toilet becomes more frequent. At times of extreme fear, the best of us can lose the ability to hold on and wetting occurs – thus the driver or pilot about to crash may wet him or her self.

Holding ability depends on the amount of urine the bladder can hold before it begins to contract, and stops adjusting its size to accommodate more urine. This point is the 'functional bladder capacity'. It is known that in many who wet the bed, bladder contractions are stronger and more frequent than they are in other people, and this point may therefore be reached with relatively little urine in the bladder. In many children with a daytime wetting problem, the pelvic floor muscles too easily allow the bladder outlet to open slightly – particularly when under the physical stress of actions such as coughing. This reduces the ability to hold on to urine, partly by allowing urine to leak out and thus wetting to occur, and partly because once urine enters the urethra (the outlet tube leading from the bladder), a sensation of urgency is felt and the flow of urine will tend to keep going.

2. *Keeping the rectum empty*
Keeping control of the bladder and of the bowel requires opposite skills. Whereas holding on to urine, within reasonable limits, is important to bladder control, controlling the bowel requires that the rectum (see **Figure 3**) is normally kept empty, and that it is emptied by defaecation shortly after the urge to empty it is felt. It is important therefore *not* to hold on to faeces for long periods after feeling the urge to defaecate, and to establish a regular bowel function through regularity of toilet visits. In normally regular bowel functioning, the rectum will fill up at fairly predictable intervals which are convenient for emptying by defaecation into the toilet.

3. *Knowing when to empty*

Controlling both the bladder and the bowel needs the individual to notice the urge to empty and, when the urge is felt, to respond in the appropriate way, within a reasonable amount of time. The urge to urinate comes from bladder contractions, and the urge to defaecate from the filling and stretching of the rectum. Different people actually feel quite different sensations of urgency to urinate, in slightly different parts of the body. Usually, the body learns to notice urgency early enough for the ability to 'hold on' until a toilet is reached. But when a toilet or some other suitable place cannot be reached within the normal holding time (as perhaps on a journey or during certain school activities), holding ability can run out and wetting then occurs.

Our perception of urgency, like other skills in staying continent, can be very much affected by outside influences. Embarrassment can make one's urge to urinate effectively disappear when other people are around at the time one is trying to urinate (for example, in hospital wards or when a doctor asks for a urine specimen). Urgency can become much less, or not felt at all, when a child is engrossed in some distracting activity, and it can be triggered or increased by thinking about visiting the toilet. Walking towards, or seeing, a toilet has the power in most of us to trigger or increase our urgency to urinate. It is a common experience for urgency to increase dramatically as the toilet is approached, particularly if we are near the limits of our ability to 'hold on', so that sometimes we only just make it. This urgency-response when we are near a toilet is very important, because it serves as a reminder to urinate if necessary when the opportunity is there, and therefore avoid possible problems later.

4. *Starting the urine stream*

Humans are almost the only animal species capable of voluntarily starting the process of emptying the bladder when it is less than full. The skill, as we have seen, is complex, involving the co-ordinated use of the muscles of the pelvic floor, diaphragm and abdomen. The factors that affect urgency also affect the ability to start the stream of urine flowing when we want it to. Most people find it difficult to start the stream when other people are around. Boys will know that it is sometimes difficult to 'go' if someone else is near you in a public toilet. In addition, the ability to start is in turn affected by anything that affects the main groups of muscles involved, for example after an operation.

A very young child empties his or her bladder whenever it is full (that is, when it has filled up to his 'functional bladder capacity'), but as the child grows older the requirements of normal bladder control make it necessary to learn how to start the urine stream at lower levels of filling than this, so that he or she can make use of toilets when they are available. Fortunately, it is rare for any child to experience difficulty in learning how to start urine flowing voluntarily – there is no need for any training beyond encouragement, opportunity and praise for success.

5. Starting defaecation

Bowel control relies heavily upon the lower bowel working to a regular routine. A key to the establishment of regular and controllable bowel function is regular defaecation, and regular emptying of the rectum in turn encourages the body to establish a similarly regular pattern of filling the rectum.

Starting defaecation, just as starting urination, requires the effective co-ordinated use of pelvic floor, diaphragm and abdominal muscles in order to put pressure where it is needed, and to allow the faeces to pass through to the outside of the body. In addition, the anus must be relaxed to open the outlet of the rectum, the anus being an integral part of the pelvic floor.

Defaecation can be affected by outside influences, in much the same way as urination. Just as with urination, defaecation can be inhibited, and the urge to empty the bowel can disappear, when other people are there. Defaecation can also easily be affected by physical factors. Constipation can make it difficult, or even painful, to expel a large and hard mass of faeces, needing a great deal of muscular pushing down onto the rectum and a widely stretched anus to accomplish the feat. Any small splits in the anus, or piles, can hinder defaecation by making it painful even without constipation.

6. *Monitoring and responding while asleep*

Problems of bowel control at night are, fortunately, very rare. The rectum's filling and need to empty usually occur during the daytime. Problems of bladder control, and thus bedwetting (or 'nocturnal enuresis') are however very common at night. The body's ability to monitor the state of the bladder during sleep is central to staying dry at night. Where the ability to 'hold on' is low, and the bladder requires emptying during the night, it is particularly important that the body's early warning monitoring system for a full bladder should arouse the child (or adult, for that matter) early enough and completely enough for the toilet to be visited in time. As the bladders of bedwetting children are liable to frequent and fairly strong contractions throughout the night, it is all the more important that awaking from sleep should occur whenever these contractions begin to build up to a peak that is likely to result in wetting.

Most people assume that deep sleep is a major cause of bedwetting, because it might result in poor bladder monitoring at night. This is not the case, however, as research studies have shown that bedwetting occurs at various stages and levels of sleep, and not solely at the deepest. At the time of wetting, the problem is that the body is not handling its bladder signals correctly, not that it is too deeply asleep. Indeed, it is often only just below the level of wakefulness that wetting happens, regardless of whether a child is a deep sleeper or not.

Most children's bodies do automatically monitor and respond to bladder contractions during sleep, but in children who wet the bed, either the monitoring, or the body's response to it, is not strong enough. Most children will move about in the bed just before they start to wet, and their brain becomes more active than during normal sleep. This activity becomes greater as the child grows older, and it may become strong enough for some children to become dry simply as a result of growing older – they grow out of the problem without needing any special help.

For some children, the monitoring and the body's responses to it are there, but are not strong enough to do more than produce restlessness and perhaps a dream about going to the toilet (a 'toilet dream'). For others, the response is strong enough to awaken the child, but not quite strong enough to waken him or her before the worst has happened and wetting has begun, so that the child wakes in the middle of wetting, or just afterwards, to find himself in a newly wet bed. For other children, the body may not respond strongly enough to lead to complete waking.

Occasionally, a child who is only partially awakened will leave the bed in a very confused state, not conscious enough to find the toilet successfully or to be fully aware of where he or she is. The child may then automatically carry out only part of the necessary procedure, perhaps emptying his bladder in the wrong place (such as on the carpet or in some odd corner), or even starting to get dressed to go to school. It is important to recognise that the resulting accidents happen because the child's body's automatic responses are not strong enough, *not* because he or she 'can really make it if he tries, but is just not trying hard enough'. These odd actions are hardly ever deliberate, but are the result of incomplete waking. The process of holding on and waking enough to find the toilet in time is a complicated chain of events that needs plenty of notice from the bladder's early warning monitoring system during sleep.

A child cannot improve the sleep-monitoring of his or her (probably particularly active) bladder simply by trying or by being told to do so. Nevertheless, as with so much else to do with bladder and bowel control, the sleep-monitoring process does change in different circumstances. Monitoring of the bladder when sleeping in unfamiliar circumstances away from home tends to be more efficient, just as the sounds in and outside an unfamiliar bedroom are noticed more. Most of us are aware of the tendency to be more disturbed in our sleep when away from home, and to be disturbed by unfamiliar sounds such as creaking in a building, traffic on the road, animal or bird sounds, or the sound of the wind in the countryside. The brain is simply more alert to signals, and more ready to respond to them, when we are on unfamiliar territory. A useful side-effect of this for a bedwetting child is that when he or she is anywhere away from his usual bed at home, he is not only more likely to be disturbed by unfamiliar sounds, but is also more likely to respond to the signals from a full bladder as well. Thus the majority of bedwetting children wet less when staying with relatives, when they are on holiday away from home, and even when they are in hospital.

Although a child cannot by choice or effort alone improve his or her body's monitoring of the bladder during sleep, his body can be trained by the enuresis alarm (described on pp. 48–60) to monitor the bladder more efficiently, selecting quite automatically for special attention the signals concerning contractions from the bladder. Signals which the brain has learned to attend to can produce an automatic response, even during the unconsciousness of sleep. The brain will, for instance, react during sleep to a tape-recording of a person's name, but not to the equally loud but meaningless sound of the same tape-recording played backwards.

7. *Knowing when and where to 'go'*
Adults who have ever wondered for a moment what to do with a bidet, or one of those continental 'footstep' toilets, will appreciate how a very young child feels when faced with different kinds of toilet. He or she must learn first that it is his potty, and not the room it is in or anything else, that is his 'go-ahead' for urination or defaecation. Then he must learn that various toilets and other places can be used as well. There are however many confusing aspects to this that also have to be learned – some toilets are reserved for 'staff' or for one sex only, and it is by no means always clear what is a toilet and what is not; chemical toilets in the ground, and many toilets

in other people's houses or public buildings are very different from the potty or toilet at home. There are some places that can be used on some occasions but not on others – thus one can 'go' behind a tree when away from a proper toilet, but not when it is just outside a house or near a toilet. Boys must learn that one does not urinate in public – except, of course, in a gentlemen's public lavatory, where you just pretend everyone else is not there. Knowing when and where one may go is not innate, but a skill that has to be acquired when very young.

8. *Coping with clothing, cleaning and toilet equipment*
Going to the toilet without help demands a range of supplementary 'coping' skills in addition to bladder and bowel control.

With any complicated skill, those who can do it will tend to forget how many separate elements are involved. An adult can easily think of 'going to the toilet' as if it were a single act, just as the experienced car driver can think of driving off in the car as a single act, forgetting the separate elements of using the ignition, accelerator, clutch, gears, steering, brakes and indicators. The child does not just 'visit the toilet'. After feeling the urge to go, he or she must hold on until he finds the right time to go and reach the toilet; he must open and close doors as necessary, raise or lower a lavatory seat (and they don't all stay where you put them!), adjust clothing as necessary (uncovering the right bits and keeping the rest of one's clothing out of the way), stand or sit in the right position (depending on sex) to avoid making a mess (boys needing to decide whether to stand or sit, and to aim straight when urinating), cleanse as necessary, readjust clothing, flush the toilet (and flushing systems vary enormously, most needing a different knack to achieve results, often being difficult to use and some requiring considerable strength), wash hands, and return to the company of everyone else without being accidentally wet, soiled, or improperly dressed.

Learning the skills – taught or just acquired?

Before each of the skills described can be used to help the child to stay clean and dry, two conditions must be met. Firstly, the body must have developed sufficiently for it to be possible for the muscles and nervous system to perform the necessary actions. Secondly, the physical skills must be developed and moulded through a process of learning, involving the association of one thing with another, the shaping of actions and reactions according to their pleasant or unpleasant consequences, and by imitation of the examples set by others.

Clearly, most of the skills of continence involve learning by the child. 'Holding' actions by the body must become associated with early signals of urgency coming from the bladder or bowel, and are encouraged by the body's natural tendency to learn responses which help it to avoid unpleasant consequences like becoming dirty, wet and cold. Holding actions are also encouraged by being associated with pleasant consequences like praise for successful toileting. One possible reason for boys having more incontinence problems than girls is that boys' skins are less sensitive to the unpleasantness of being wet and cold – one factor likely to encourage the necessary learning. The efficient use of the pelvic floor muscles in holding on, and in starting both urination and defaecation, has to be learned, as does the use of the pelvic floor muscles, diaphragm and abdominal muscles. The link between strong bladder contractions while asleep and the two reactions of holding on and waking up also has to be learned.

The question arises as to whether all this needs to be *taught* to the child, or whether it will be learned quite naturally. A number of points may be made in answer. Firstly, some of the learning involved – such as the co-ordination of various internal muscles – is so complex that no parent could possibly teach it to a child, any more than one could teach a child what he must do to raise his arm. These bodily skills are usually learned without help. It is interesting to note that many children show that they have learned, without being taught, that lifting the pelvic floor reduces urgency, when they press it upwards by sitting on a heel or a hard edge. Secondly, a large proportion of the necessary learning is known to occur quite naturally, without teaching, provided that all the normal opportunities for learning and practice are available. Thirdly, some of the learning does require encouragement, although formal teaching or training is more than is needed for most children. Thus parents need to help to introduce the child to the idea of a potty or toilet, give appropriate opportunities for the child to become familiar with using it, and to encourage and praise even small steps of success in *any* of the basic skills of control that have been outlined – certainly for 'producing' in the potty, but also for the less obvious skills like success at holding on to urine for a while, and coping with clothing.

Learning bladder and bowel control is very similar to learning to speak. In learning speech, the complex bodily movements needed to produce the sounds *are* learned, but cannot be taught by the average parent. Opportunity to hear and practise speech is needed, praise for success is given, and some guidance is needed with the unfamiliar.

All learning can be held back or broken up, even when complete, by serious stress, and the learning of bladder and bowel control is no exception. Children who experience major changes or serious stresses in their lives when aged two to three years (which is when they are doing most of their learning of continence) are more likely than others to have difficulties with bladder or bowel control. In addition to this, it must be emphasised that the skills of control are not equally easy for all children (or adults), any more than the skills of playing the piano or driving a car are equally easy for all, and some children find these skills sufficiently difficult to have major problems in learning them. Some children are also more sensitive to their learned skills, such as bladder and bowel control, being disrupted or destroyed by stress.

Most readers of this book will have come across either the failure or the breakdown of bladder or bowel control. Stress, or a difficulty which can be inherited, in the complicated skills concerned with continence may well be involved, and training in the problematic skills, as described in later chapters, is required to remedy the situation. However, failure or breakdown of continence is *not* likely to result from any lack of formal toilet training in early childhood.

Toilet training and its effects

Having noted that the most useful form of toilet training is likely to consist of a 'helping hand' with opportunities, guidance and praise, rather than any formal training course, it is also worth noting that most parents start too early and are probably too formal over toilet training. A major British research study of child upbringing reported that one in five mothers had started 'training' before their children were two months old, two thirds by eight months, and over eight out of ten by the child's first birthday. For most children, training at any time in the first year is asking too much of his or her physical maturity, and the child is simply not physically capable of performing many of the necessary actions.

The following sections outline some of the more common toilet training techniques:

1. *Daytime potting*

Potting the child during the day is the most common form of toilet training. Its effect is overrated, nevertheless. Research studies have found it to have little beneficial effect upon either daytime or night-time wetting. Its potential disadvantage is that if it becomes a source of stress and conflict between parents and child (as it can so easily), it can slow down the natural learning of control. Potting does however help with bowel control to some extent, although children who are not potted soon catch up with those that are.

From what has already been said about the various elements of control, it is clear that learning to produce urine or faeces in the pot is a relatively small part of the overall skill of continence. Potting gives a temporary lead in bowel control because it helps to keep the rectum in its normal empty state, in which it is most sensitive to the stretch-effect of faeces entering it. Because the bladder, on the other hand, is quite a different design and needs to become adjusted to holding on to urine for reasonable periods rather than frequently emptying, emptying the bladder into a pot has little effect on the vital holding ability. It does probably help in learning how to start urinating at will, and in learning one acceptable place in which to urinate.

Potting is likely to be helpful to some extent, but it is a great deal of effort for relatively little gain, and children not potted will usually do just as well in the long run.

2. Night-time potting or 'lifting'

Many parents 'lift' or wake their children at night, often when they come to bed themselves, to urinate in the toilet. As with daytime potting, lifting at night can help, but it is a lot of effort for very little benefit in many cases. It is a procedure many parents who visit bedwetting clinics have been following without results for years. If night-time lifting has been tried for six months without results, it is unlikely to be worth continuing. The child is probably either not yet sufficiently mature physically for night-time control, or the technique is not an effective one for him or her. It may be tried again, for a similar period, a year or so later.

The problem with night lifting is that, while it does at least mean some urine is in the toilet rather than the bed, it does not teach or train the child to develop his or her own bodily control. The child does not learn to associate waking up with the feeling of a full bladder, because his bladder is unlikely to be full or starting to contract just at the point when his parents lift or wake him. Night lifting can also produce some odd effects on rare occasions. I have come across children at my clinics who have learned to empty their bladders when they hear someone approaching at night, because they have learned to associate these events. Others, if lifting is for some reason stopped, will wet at what has become the usual time, having learned to rely

23

on parental help rather than body control to stay dry. These odd effects can be reduced by lifting at irregular times and avoiding following a similar routine each night, so that it does not encourage regular reactions in the child's body or reliance on one aspect or another of the lifting routine.

3. Encouragement and praise

Immediately praising a child for any success, and even for a sign of progress, is one of the best forms of help a parent can give. It is not a training 'routine', but a matter of watching out for each small step and praising it. This encourages toilet control in exactly the same way as it assists walking when first steps are noticed and praised, or talking when first words are picked out and responded to. Much research into toilet training and the learning of other skills has demonstrated how powerful immediate praise can be, and it is important to note that all learning is more efficient when it is encouraged and reinforced by praise. Progress should be looked for in each of the basic skills already described, not just in 'producing' in the potty. To praise a child for holding urine and staying dry, even for short periods at first, is equally important.

4. Punishment

Many parents punish children for 'accidents', at the same time as they are following a potting routine. Accidents must be expected, and while praise for success effectively 'seals' the learning in a little more firmly each time, punishment of failures does *not* help the child to become clean or dry. Where an 'accident' is simply a matter of not having enough skill, punishment is probably useless. And it is worth remembering, when a child soils or wets just after refusing an opportunity to 'go', that knowing when you need to go is a skill to be learned like the others.

5. Changes in circumstances

Where a child has almost achieved control, a major change like coming out of nappies, having 'grown-up' clothes or pyjamas, or changing beds or bedrooms, will often be enough to tip the balance towards full control. The danger, of course, is in making such a change when the child is not ready, and then being disappointed when he or she fails to achieve success.

6. Restricting drinking

Drinking should not be restricted as a toilet-training technique. The less full bladder is not likely to empty less, except for the period immediately after the start of fluid restrictions. All that happens is that the bladder adjusts to holding less urine (its 'functional capacity', as already described, reduces), so that the bladder performs all its usual actions of producing feelings of urgency, and of emptying, but when less full than before. The ability to hold on to urine, which is central to bladder control, is thus impaired, and bladder control can actually be *reduced* by restricting a child's drinking.

7. Demonstration

Children need to learn how to cope with toilets and clothing, and much of this is learned by watching others and simply being shown what to do. Demonstrating each stage, with less help being needed as the child begins to pick up the skill for himself or herself, and with praise to seal in any progress made, is as powerful a form of toilet-training as most children need, or can benefit from.

Some special intensive 'programmes' of toilet-training are now available in book form. These are highly formal procedures, usually based on the idea of immediate and intensive praise for success and perhaps remedial training for failure. They may be regarded as a concentrated focusing of commonsense and effective techniques to accelerate the natural learning of bladder and bowel control. Some use alarm devices worn in the underclothes to signal wetting to the child's parents – this helps the parents to know when to praise holding on, and in effect to stop the wetting in its tracks while the child is taken to the toilet. Another, designed by Dr Azrin and his colleagues in America (see **Further Reading** on p. 168), involves increased drinking, very frequent toileting, extensive praise for both 'producing' in the toilet and for remaining clean and dry, and prolonged practice of toileting, with reprimands for accidents. Guidance on dressing and adjusting clothing is included.

Such intensive training has been found effective when properly carried out, but it does demand very great effort and determination on the part of all concerned, and has to be followed strictly, which not all parents find easy or pleasant. These programmes are particularly useful when experienced professional supervision is available, and in some special circumstances, as for example where only intensive training can help a handicapped child, or where for some reason it is more than usually important for a child to become clean and dry quickly.

A number of toilet-training 'aids' are nowadays on the market, including potties that play tunes when filled. This is another variation on the theme of praise for success, although it must again be said that learning to stay clean and dry involves many more skills than simply 'producing' in the potty. It is also a very expensive way indeed of praising a child, when parents can praise or reward a child equally well or better by themselves!

Conclusion – encouraging control

The key words in toilet-training are *opportunity*, *encouragement*, and *praise*. One should not expect anything to happen towards becoming clean and dry until around the middle of the second year of life (much later than most parents start trying to toilet-train their children), when there are the first signs that the child knows that urination or defaecation is about to happen. They perhaps clutch at themselves and hold on to urine for just a moment, and they might show a dislike of being wet or soiled. At this point introduction to the idea of a potty (but not necessarily regular potting) and the opportunity to use it at the right time, are appropriate.

Parents should try to notice even very small steps in each of the toileting skills already described, praising and perhaps occasionally rewarding their child, but expecting the frequent setbacks that happen in the early stages of learning anything. No one (even an adult) suddenly acquires full competence in learning any skill; it takes a long time to become an expert, whether at playing the piano or controlling urine. Success at holding on and in coping with clothing should be noticed and praised, just as much as successful urination or bowel movements in the pot. At an appropriate point nappies need to be left off for a period, and frequent accidents during this changeover are inevitable. In the case of a mentally handicapped child, a systematic 'programme' of encouragement and praise, as described in Chapter Eight, has been found effective for many.

Toilet training is taken too seriously by most people. The vast majority of children, with a very simple 'helping hand' as just outlined, will become clean and dry as naturally as they learn to speak, and children who are not 'trained' become just as continent as those who are. Lack of formal toilet-training does not cause wetting or soiling, and the child with a wetting or soiling problem would probably have had the same problem regardless of his or her parents' training.

THREE

THE PROBLEM OF BEDWETTING

Nature and frequency

Whether a bed is wet or not is relatively easy to determine. Whether a particular child should be considered to be a bedwetter is, however, not so clear. How often wetting happens, how long it continues, and the child's age must all be taken into account. Bedwetting (or 'nocturnal enuresis') may be defined as 'persistent and frequent urination during sleep at an age at which a greater degree of night-time bladder control is considered to be normal'. Many children (and not a few adults) have the occasional wet bed, and in most cases this need be of little concern. The 'occasional accident' may be regarded as potential 'bedwetting' when it is frequent and persistent enough to be a major problem.

Deliberate wetting

Many parents wonder whether perhaps the bedwetting child is just basically lazy, and could be dry if only he or she wished. This, however, is extremely unlikely to be the case. The number of children who regularly and deliberately wet the bed when awake is almost negligible.

Many parents will have noticed that their usually bedwetting child tends to wet less, or not at all, when sleeping away from home – on holiday, perhaps, or when staying with relatives. It is all too easy to interpret this as evidence of some element of choice by the child in whether or not to be wet. This is not the case. Wetting is in fact very, and quite automatically, sensitive to changes in surroundings. Just as one is more aware of, and more easily awoken by, outside sounds when sleeping in unfamiliar surroundings, so one is also more aware of, and more easily woken by, the functioning of one's own body. The body's awareness of bladder activity increases when sleeping in unusual surroundings, as if the brain is more actively on 'sentry duty' when away from home. It is surprising, but common, that a bedwetting child may wet less than usual, or not at all, when under the stress of being in hospital.

How many children wet the bed?
Bedwetting tends to clear up as children grow older. The decrease in the number of bedwetters with increasing age is greatest amongst younger children. There is no sudden tendency to become dry at puberty. If one were to take 100 bedwetting children aged between 5 and 19, one would expect between 13 and 16 of them to become dry within one year without any special treatment, simply because they have grown older. There is however no guarantee, and no way of telling, whether any particular child or young person is going to grow out of the problem without treatment. Each bedwetting child or young person has about a one in seven chance every year of being lucky enough to grow out of it without help.

The number of children one would define as bedwetters depends upon the frequency of wetting one picks as constituting bedwetting as opposed to the occasional accident. However, when research studies using various frequencies as the definition are put together, frequent and persistent bedwetting has been found to be a problem for approximately 11 per cent of all 5 year olds, 7 per cent of 7 year olds, 5 per cent of 10 year olds, and between 1 and 2 per cent of those over 15 – including adults. These figures are illustrated in **Figure 4**. The problem of bedwetting is higher than most children, and most parents, realise. It is worth saying to a ten-year-old worried by his or her bedwetting that even though he may not know about anyone else having the same problem, he is unlikely to be the only one with the problem amongst classmates at school.

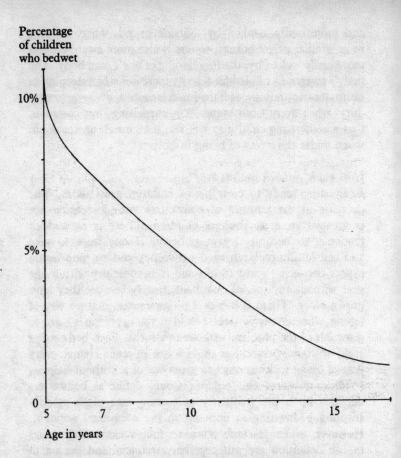

Fig.4　The frequency of bedwetting

Sex Ratio

Approximately twice as many boys as girls have a bedwetting problem, and boys tend to become dry at night slightly later than girls. There are many theories as to why this is so. The fact already mentioned that boys' skins are rather less sensitive to the feelings of being wet and cold, probably plays a part in the natural learning of bladder control. Boys do tend to have more 'developmental' problems than girls anyway – more boys than girls have problems learning to read, for example.

Social class

Fewer children of 'professional' families tend to have a bed-wetting problem than the children of 'unskilled' parents. The difference is particularly marked amongst older children and amongst bedwetting girls.

The beginning of the problem

Between eight and nine out of ten bedwetting children (and most adult bedwetters) are lifelong (or 'primary') bedwetters, never having been reliably dry for a significant period. Those who lose their night-time bladder control after a reasonable period of dryness are often termed 'secondary' bedwetters. There is, however, little agreement on just how long one has to have been dry to qualify as a 'secondary' bedwetter, and the child who has never been consistently dry has basically the same problem as the child who has lost his or her previous control, even after a number of years. The one has found control hard to achieve, while the other has only just managed to achieve it but has not been able to hold onto it, perhaps in the face of some major change or stress. Both are likely to respond to the same treatments in the same way.

Bedwetting in families

Problems of bladder control tend to run in families, and there is evidence that difficulty in gaining or holding on to bladder control can to some extent be inherited. About two out of three bedwetting children have a close relative who has, or had, the same problem. Some parents of bedwetters will therefore remember having had the same problem themselves in their own childhood, or will come across it in other children of the family or among relatives. It seems that bladder control problems must be expected amongst some members, and in each generation, of families where bladder control happens to be a hard skill to get and to keep. I find it helpful to tell children worried about their own wetting, that there are likely

31

to be relatives in their parents' generation who had exactly the same problem as children, and that the chances are that when they are parents themselves in the future, they are very likely to find the problem occurring among their own children as well. This helps to put the problem into perspective.

The origins of bedwetting

It is probable that any one child's bedwetting has a number of factors contributing to it, rather than being produced by any single, easily identifiable cause. The following list gives some of the more common factors that one may come across:

Emotional stress

Both failure to achieve full bladder control in the first place, and its loss once gained, are often linked to some major change or stress in the child's life. There is research evidence that stresses and anxieties in the third or fourth year of a child's life may result in bedwetting, and stresses such as the family breaking up, problems at school, moving house, or the birth of a new brother or sister can disrupt any bladder control that has already been gained. The same stresses will not trigger bedwetting in all children, but some children are particularly sensitive to certain forms of stress, and bladder control is a particularly difficult and insecure skill for some children.

Once bladder control has been disrupted, it may return naturally with time, but very often special treatment will be necessary to restore it. Bedwetting is of course in itself a source of anxiety and stress which can create a vicious circle by hindering the very learning necessary to regain the skills of control. The stress that prevented control or triggered bedwetting has very often long passed – even a brief period of stress at the age of two or three can leave a child with a wetting problem for years, and the 'secondary' bedwetting that starts after a period of dryness can remain long after any triggering stress has passed and been forgotten. Bedwetting tends to be at its most persistent when there are family difficulties.

In helping a child or young person with a bedwetting problem, it is worth checking whether there is still some major source of stress which may be making learning difficult. Sorting out this stress (if it is possible to do so) will help to make control more possible, and improve the child's response to any special treatments for bedwetting. It is also worthwhile sorting out a stress for its own sake, if possible. However, if no present stress is obvious to you, there is no point in spending ages trying to find one – if you and the child have to search your minds to think of a possible stress, it is not likely to be a relevant one, and it is more than likely that if any stress or change was relevant once, it has long since gone.

'Individual differences'

There are a great many differences, partly inherited, between children in the ease with which they acquire and keep bladder control. For some, full and permanent control seems to emerge quickly and effortlessly, whereas others have serious problems. Bedwetting can be caused by little more than the fact that a child happens to find the skills of control difficult. Children differ in the ease with which they learn complex physical skills like swimming or riding a bicycle, and they differ just as much with other physical skills like bladder or bowel control.

Infection

Bedwetting can be triggered by an infection in the urinary system (some 16 per cent of children with such an infection wet the bed), and wetting in its turn increases the possibility of an infection occurring. Both boys and girls can have an infection as well as bedwetting, but it is more likely for girls, whose urethra (the outlet of the tube from the bladder) is more easily entered by infection-causing organisms. The majority of bedwetting children are free of such an infection, but about one in twenty bedwetting girls may be expected to have one. Because of the possibility of infection, a doctor should be consulted in all cases of persistent bedwetting. He or she is able to check for infection by sending a urine sample to be examined in the laboratory. Any infection that is found can usually be cured simply through a course of antibiotic tablets. Infections need to be treated as problems in their own right, and removing them will help to relieve the wetting. However, other specific treatment of the wetting is still needed for about 70 per cent of bedwetting children with an infection. Usually the treatment of wetting and the antibiotic treatments can be carried out at the same time. Where a girl has repeated infections, it is worth checking with her that when she has emptied her bowels she is cleaning herself from front to back, and not the other way round. Wiping herself from back to front will wipe infecting organisms over her urethra.

Abnormalities
Very few children or young people wet the bed because of any physical abnormality – far fewer than most children and their parents might fear. A doctor should be asked to check any bedwetting child physically so that the slight possibility of an abnormality can be ruled out (or, in the rare cases where something *is* found, it can be investigated and treated if it needs to be). In the vast majority of cases, the physical check will result in reassurance that all is well. Where a slight physical abnormality is found, it may nevertheless be that one of the basic treatments for bedwetting will still be appropriate and successful. Even where there is a major abnormality, the same basic treatments may help to improve bladder control to some extent. But in all cases involving some physical abnormality, the doctor's assessment of the suitability of one of the basic bedwetting treatments is essential.

Contrary to popular belief, bedwetting in boys has nothing to do with whether he has been circumcised or not, and is not caused by undescended testicles.

Many people regard bedwetting as being caused by a 'weak bladder', but this idea does not explain a great deal, as the crucial factor in the bladder's ability to hold urine is its functional capacity (the level of filling at which bladder contractions and urgency begin), and this is capable of quite marked changes. It has little to do with the 'strength' or 'weakness' of the bladder itself. Children who wet the bed do not usually have small bladders, but they do tend to have bladders that start the emptying process when they are not very full, and about one in two bedwetting children have overactive bladders. However, weakness of the pelvic floor muscles between the legs would be important, as it may result in failure to keep the bladder's outlet raised and closed.

Deep sleep

Contrary to an almost universal belief, bedwetting has virtually nothing to do with deep sleep. Research has established that bedwetting happens at all stages and depths of sleep (except during dreaming sleep), and not at just the deepest. The 'toilet dreams' experienced by some children, in which they dream they are at the toilet when actually wetting in the bed, are not dreams which lead to urination, but the other way around – the dream is triggered by a wetting which has failed to waken the child, just registering in his or her consciousness sufficiently to affect dreaming. Not surprisingly, drugs aimed at nothing more than lightening sleep have not proved effective treatments for bedwetting. Children who wet the bed do not usually have a sleep pattern that is any different from that of dry children.

Emotional disturbance

Bedwetting is regarded by some as an expression of some deep emotional disturbance, and any treatment therefore needs to deal with the disturbance that is assumed to be there, rather than with the bedwetting as such. It is sometimes described as a 'safety valve' for psychological disturbance, or thought to indicate that the child has suffered some form of distressing experience.

It is certainly true that more bedwetters than dry children have emotional problems. However, three vital points need to be made on this issue. Firstly, although *more* bedwetters than others have emotional problems, the *majority* of bedwetters are

35

nevertheless psychologically completely normal. Secondly, it is not surprising that bedwetting and emotional problems come together in some children, since both can be caused by the same factors – for example, stresses in the family. Thirdly, bedwetting is in itself a source of stress which can actually cause emotional problems. The fact that a child may not have learned (or kept) full bladder control because his or her learning of the necessary skills has been disrupted by stresses, is *not* the same thing as the bedwetting being part of some wider emotional problem. We all learn badly when under stress, but that does not mean that we are emotionally disturbed.

It is not appropriate to consider a child as disturbed simply because he or she wets the bed, nor to assume that the bedwetting proves that there has been any particular form of distressing experience or type of stress in the child's life. One should not assume that bedwetting in some way *needs* to be there to serve as a safety valve. Some people worry that if bedwetting itself is cured by some specific form of treatment, disturbance will then show itself in some other way and something else will go wrong – perhaps another problem will emerge to take the place of the safety valve that has been removed. Careful research into the subject however has shown clearly that no such problem does emerge when bedwetting is treated directly. Bedwetting can be treated directly and in its own right as nothing more nor less than poor bladder control, without the fear that it may be an emotional safety valve, or that its removal will affect anything else.

It is also important to emphasize that bedwetting does not suggest that a child has suffered from sexual abuse: a vast variety of factors can trigger a loss of bladder control and the physical closeness of urinary and sexual organs does not mean that there is any connection between wetting and sexual problems or abuse.

It is very helpful and reassuring to many children with a bedwetting problem to explain that it does not mean that they are psychologically disturbed, babyish or immature and that it may simply be nothing more complicated than that finding bladder control hard to learn runs in the family (just as being tall or short can run in the family). Being poor at learning bladder control does not mean that one has emotional problems, any more than being poor at swimming or gymnastics does.

Common ways of helping the bedwetting child

Many parents coping with a child's bedwetting problem will have come across one or more of the following approaches, some based on toilet-training strategies already described.

Lifting at night

Waking the child at night to visit the toilet has been noted in Chapter Two as a common but not highly effective form of toilet-training. Parents of older children have often tried lifting, without results, for a number of years. As we have already seen, lifting rarely improves control, even if it does keep some urine from the bed, and it can teach a child to rely on being woken and even (though rarely) to wet automatically in response to household sounds like someone coming upstairs or into the bedroom. If lifting is to be used, it is best to vary the times that one wakes the child, and to avoid following a standard routine. Do not always lift the child at your own regular bedtime, but vary as much as possible the time between the child going off to sleep and you waking him or her to use the toilet, making sure that there is at least an hour's difference between one night and the next. Avoid waking the child in the same way each night; where both parents are available, one can do the waking one night, the other on another night. Wake the child with the light on sometimes, and off at others, and use different ways of waking. The object is to avoid there being any routine which might become connected to emptying the bladder automatically.

An irregularly-timed and non-routine programme of lifting

is certainly worth trying, and is an easy form of DIY treatment, but it is not likely to improve bladder control if it has not done so within six months. Keep a record of wet and dry nights while trying it, and if it is achieving an improvement then keep going.

Punishment

Punishing a child for wetting the bed does not improve matters. It is understandable that many parents may lose patience at times, but it does not help. Praising or rewarding successes has more effect in the development of bladder control (or any other skill being learned, for that matter) than punishment for mistakes or failures.

The different effects of praise and punishment for a child learning bladder control are rather like those that might be experienced by a learner driver trying to change gear. The driver is more likely to succeed if smooth gear changes (however rare they are at first!) are noticed and praised, than if every jerky or noisy gear change produces criticism or exasperation from the instructor.

Rewards

Rewarding successes will help the development of bladder control both in older children and during the development of control in infancy. By keeping a record of wet and dry nights, any progress can be noticed (gradual progress is often unnoticed without some form of record to compare results). Rewarding success is known from a vast amount of research work to be more effective in developing skills than the punishment of failures, and it is most effective if it is immediate. So it is far better to give a word of congratulation or a small reward for each dry night, or each waking to visit the toilet, or the achievement of a target like two or three dry nights in a row, than to promise something like a new bicycle when the child becomes completely dry. Praise is as good a reward as any, but the occasional tangible reward as a celebration of progress made can usefully be added.

It is important to stress that the fact that praise or rewards can improve learning does *not* imply that the child could 'do it if he tried'. The learning of all skills is more efficient if successes are rewarded, and celebration of actual progress made is not at all the same thing as bribery!

Record charts and 'star charts'

Starting to keep a record chart of wet and dry nights is a useful first move to help a child with wetting that is too infrequent for more specific treatments such as drugs or an enuresis alarm. It serves a dual purpose by helping to reduce wetting, and by showing exactly how often wetting is occurring and whether it is getting worse or better. This is not always easy to tell with occasional and irregular wetting.

Keeping a systematic record of wet and dry nights does have the effect for some children of reducing their wetting. Keeping a record pinpoints successes and focuses positive consequences onto any small steps forward that are made. Simply keeping a record chart (such as the one illustrated in **Figure 10**, see p. 72) can, unlikely as it may sound, help to reduce wetting; and it is all the better if it can be the child rather than a parent who fills in the chart. Even if an adult has to fill in the chart, it is important that the child knows what is being written on it each morning, and looks after his or her own chart.

A record of wet and dry nights can be converted into a reward system for a younger child, by using it as a 'star chart' on which he or she can place stick-on stars for dry nights (see **Figure 5**). The reward effect of stars can be reinforced with praise and the occasional 'back-up' tangible reward. With an older child or young person, a straightforward wet and dry record chart can have the same positive effect by pinpointing successes.

Restriction of drinking

From the earlier description of the way the bladder functions (see Chapter Two), it is clear that fluid restriction as a way of

39

A star chart

Name________________________

Starting date________________________

Weeks

	1	2	3	4	5	6	7	8	9	10	11	12
Monday												
Tuesday												
Wednesday												
Thursday												
Friday												
Saturday												
Sunday												

Put a 'W' for a wet night

Draw or stick a star for a dry night

Fig.5 Star chart

trying to control bedwetting is based on a misconception, and does not help. Wetting is not a problem of the bladder becoming too full. The problem is that the body is not responding appropriately, or soon enough or strongly enough, when the bladder begins to contract ready to empty. The amount of urine the bladder is prepared to hold before this happens can be changed by the various factors described earlier on, and one of these is the amount of fluid drunk (and thus the amount of urine produced for the bladder to hold).

Some children do tend to wet more after particular kinds of drink. Of course, avoiding 'problem types' of drink can help reduce the problem in such cases, but the object of any treatment needs to be to enable the child to cope without having to avoid particular drinks.

Cutting down on drinking can, unfortunately, appear to help at first, but only until the bladder begins to adjust to the lower fluid intake. After that, fluid restriction can *reduce* bladder control by reducing the ability to hold onto urine. A bedwetting child should be allowed to drink when thirsty, even if this is just before bed. As will be seen in later chapters, fluid *increase*, rather than fluid *reduction* forms a part of some treatment techniques.

Common forms of treatment

When advice is sought from a doctor or other professional about bedwetting, one of the following basic courses of action is likely to be advised. Naturally, other ways of coping or helping may be suggested, and different children may need different forms of help, but the approaches outlined below are the most common and the most researched.

Before any visit to seek professional advice for a wetting or soiling problem, it is helpful to keep a record of wet and dry nights, as, unless wetting occurs every night without exception, it is very common for one's estimate of wetting frequency to be inaccurate. Also a record of wet and dry nights is needed to monitor the progress being made with any type of treatment (or, just as important, whether little or no progress is being made, suggesting a review of the approach being used and possibly a change). A record of the situation for at least two weeks before any treatment is begun provides a vital basis against which later records can be compared to measure progress. A suitable and straightforward wet and dry night record chart is illustrated in **Figure 10**, see p. 72

Reassurance

'Reassurance' has been included here because it is very often the main help offered by a doctor, particularly for bedwetting in a fairly young child. To know that there is nothing physically wrong, and that there are no signs of infection, is the very important and reassuring result of most consultations with a doctor about bedwetting, and it is certainly true that most bedwetters will grow out of the problem eventually – as has been noted, between 13 and 16 per cent will do so in each year. However, some children may take years to do so, and thus it is worth discussing some form of positive treatment wherever bedwetting is a source of distress, particularly in an older child. Knowing that a six year old has a 13 to 16 per cent chance of becoming dry without treatment within a year is quite reassuring. It is not at all comforting to a young adult who has not been one of the lucky percentage for year after year, and for whom bedwetting is affecting social life and perhaps training, employment or even boyfriend/girlfriend relationships.

Drug treatments
The use of tablets or medicine is the most common form of positive treatment for bedwetting. A number of different types of medication is available, some drugs being available in both tablet and liquid form. Commonly prescribed drugs are Tofranil, Tyrimide, Tryptizol, Cetiprin and Desmospray. Many of the drugs used work on the principle of 'dampening down' the sensitivity and activity of the bladder, reducing its tendency to contract too quickly and actively once it reaches the first stages of urgency, and also increasing its functional capacity, and thus the child's ability to 'hold on'. A number of these drugs also have other effects, and are used in the treatment of other and often quite different problems; some, for example, are also used for the treatment of depression in adults. In all cases, drugs used to treat bedwetting should be used strictly in accordance with the doctor's instructions. As with any drugs, a higher dosage than has been prescribed can be dangerous.

An increasingly widely used medication for bedwetting is desmopressin, or 'Desmospray'. This is a nasal spray containing an artificial version of the natural hormone called vasopressin. Vasopressin reduces the amount of urine that the kidneys produce, and our bodies naturally make vasopressin to help night-time control by slowing our urine production down when we are asleep. Treatment with Desmospray at night strengthens this effect, helping the body to produce less urine at night and so make it easier for the body's controls to cope without wetting.

Because there are a number of drugs that might be suitable, it is well worth recording progress with any that are prescribed (using the type of chart shown in **Figure 10**, see p. 72), and visiting the doctor again to ask his or her advice on a possible change of drug or dosage if a particular prescription does not appear to be working.

There is one drawback with drug treatments for bedwetting, whichever drug is used, and that is the tendency for wetting to start again once the medication has been stopped. This is mainly because the drugs do not directly train the body to increase control, nor do they have a permanent 'dampening down' effect on the bladder after being stopped. They may, however, in some cases reduce the problem while the body's own control develops enough to take over, and they can reduce the unhelpful stress and anxiety of continued wetting. Drugs can be expected to produce a lasting cure in about one in five cases, and they are useful in the short term in suppressing wetting for a period when it matters more than usual (perhaps reducing wet nights on holiday, or at times of stress). They are certainly useful, even if they may not produce permanent bladder control, when parents feel they cannot cope with continued wetting without seriously losing their temper and ability to stay sympathetic. Drug treatment also has the distinct advantage that it is easier and not stressful to use compared with the more effective, but also more demanding, 'alarm' treatment described in later chapters.

Psychotherapy

As has already been discussed, although opinions differ widely on whether bedwetting is linked to emotional disturbance, it seems safe and effective to treat bedwetting as a problem on its own, without fear of causing problems by removing some

43

kind of safety valve from the child.

Psychotherapy treatments, involving play therapy or talk-ing things through with a therapist, are sometimes used for bedwetting, on the basis that if there should be any underlying emotional problem, this approach is likely to sort it out and so help with the bedwetting. However, research studies that have compared these treatments with more direct approaches (such as the 'enuresis alarm' described below and on pp. 48–60) that are aimed at increasing bodily control over the bladder, have shown that the psychotherapy treatments have little effect on bedwetting. This again indicates that bedwetting is best regarded as nothing more nor less than poor bladder control, and not as some form of emotional disturbance.

Where a child has problems other than bedwetting, or is suffering from more general stresses and anxieties, the doctor or other professional adviser may recommend a psychotherapy treatment for these problems. If so, a treatment such as drugs or an enuresis alarm can usually be used separately for the bedwetting. Wetting can usually be treated on its own, without ill effects, whether it is the child's only major problem or one of many problems the child has.

The enuresis alarm

The enuresis alarm is sometimes also known as the 'buzzer' or the 'bell and pad' (the latter rather misleadingly, as it is many years since bells were involved!) The great weight of research conducted into the treatment of bedwetting (or enuresis) has shown the alarm to be the most effective generally available treatment. As is often the way of things, it also demands the greatest effort to produce results. Although it can provide more, and more long-lasting, cures than drug treatments, it is nothing like as easy to use, and each family considering a choice of treatments must weigh up for themselves the likely benefits and the costs in terms of effort that each approach involves. In the vast majority of cases, the enuresis alarm is likely to be more effective than psychotherapy treatment, a basic reward system or star chart, or simply waiting for a child to grow out of the problem.

The alarm is a treatment used at home by the child or young person concerned, helped and supervised by his or her parent(s). Alarms can be obtained in one of two ways: from a clinic or doctor's practice specialising in the treatment of bedwetting (if one is available locally), or by hiring or purchasing the necessary equipment directly from the manufacturer. In either case, success depends on parents and children knowing how to use the alarm properly at home at night, when outside advice is not available. Mistakes are easily made, and though they are not likely to be in any way dangerous, they will very probably reduce the chances of success.

Although the alarm is primarily used as a treatment for bedwetting in children and young people, it is just as suitable and effective as a treatment for bedwetting in adults, up to (but not including) old age. For wetting that has *begun* in old age, the alarm is not an effective treatment because the problem is then more likely to arise from one of the changes in the body as it becomes aged, like pelvic floor muscles losing their 'tone', or (in men) the prostate gland becoming enlarged and pressing on the urethra, interfering with the normal emptying of the bladder. Some sources of information on the possible causes of, and means of coping with, wetting in elderly people are listed in **Further Reading** at the end of this book.

'Dry Bed' training

This treatment approach originated in America, from the work of Azrin and his colleague psychologists working with handicapped people, and is increasingly being used in this country following a number of research reports that it has a good success rate. Dry bed training is a major variant of alarm treatment, and is basically a combination of an enuresis alarm with a very intensive skill and response training programme, involving one main night of concentrated training, with supporting procedures phasing out over the following nights of alarm use. The effectiveness of dry bed training is comparable with that of standard alarm treatment, with a similar relapse rate, but it can be faster acting. I have found a modified version of dry bed training to be useful as a 'crash course' or booster training for children who are not progressing well during a more usual course of alarm treatment (see chapter six).

There are now a number of versions of dry bed training, because different research studies have reported particular elements of the original intensive training 'package' to be more effective than others. Also, because of its intensive nature, many therapists have produced variations to fit the different circumstances of different patients. The following training methods may be used in a 'dry bed' treatment:

1. *Positive Practice*: in order to make the body really expert at getting out of bed to visit the toilet whenever necessary, so that this is likely to happen almost automatically when the bladder is preparing to empty at night, the child is asked to practice getting out of bed, going to the toilet and getting back into bed, ten times before finally settling to sleep on the main training night. This 10 times practice is also done again after the alarm is triggered by a wet bed during the training night or the following 'phasing out' nights of the treatment.

2. *Hourly waking*; during the one training night, the parents wake the child up each hour, the child gets out of bed, and the parent congratulates the child for having a dry bed (which he or she will have, otherwise the alarm would have gone off). The praise and celebration are intended to encourage the learning of whatever the body has done over the past hour to remain dry. The child is then asked whether he or she feels any need to go to the toilet, goes if he needs to, or goes back to bed if he doesn't need to visit the toilet – with more congratulations for being able to hold on.

3. *'Retention control training'*; this is simply jargon for practicing holding on to urine, and encouraging the bladder

to increase its 'functional' capacity. The child is encouraged to have a good drink before going to bed, and again if he or she can manage it at each hourly waking on the training night, so that getting used to holding more in the bladder becomes part of the intensive pattern of training.

4. *Follow up training*; after the big training night, the child continues to use the alarm normally, and is woken as above only once rather than hourly – on the first night, three hours after going to sleep, then half an hour earlier each night until the waking time is while he or she is still awake. After this, the alarm is continued in use for a period to 'catch' any wets that may still happen. If the child wets the bed during the follow up nights, setting the alarm off, the waking time is put back by one half-hour step for the next night, so that the phasing out is slowed down.

Research has found that using the alarm is an important part of dry bed training (the training is much less effective if it is tried without an alarm), and that the hourly waking is the most effective part of the treatment. Some therapists therefore leave out some parts of dry bed training, such as the 'positive practice' element. It is important to stress, however, that dry bed training is more complicated than using an alarm alone, and should therefore only be tried with the guidance of someone experienced in its use.

Because of its general effectiveness, and because it is not as simple to use as it looks, the next two chapters are devoted to giving guidance on understanding and using the enuresis alarm as a home treatment for bedwetting. The guidance given should supplement and expand on the advice received from clinic or doctor, or be the main source of guidance to parents who wish to use an alarm obtained privately.

FOUR

HOW ALARM TREATMENT WORKS

The enuresis alarm is a device used to treat bedwetting by training the body to respond quickly and appropriately to a full bladder during sleep.

The treatment was never invented – it was discovered by accident. The idea of a device which woke a bedwetting child up the moment he began to wet was put forward as long ago as 1830, but there is no evidence that it was ever tried out in practice. Then, in 1904, a German physician named Pfaundler devised an alarm system for a quite different purpose. He installed alarms on the beds in his children's wards in hospital, in order to alert nurses when a child had wet the bed so that the bed could be changed and the child given dry clothing as quickly as possible. He discovered that for some reason the children's bedwetting reduced as a result. Even then, it was another 34 years before this discovery was turned into a treatment for bedwetting, when Mowrer and Mowrer developed it and tried it out, with excellent results they published in 1938. Today's alarm treatment is basically the same as that pioneered by the Mowrers, but with far more sophisticated alarm devices, and with much more known about how best to use the equipment and overcome the inevitable problems in any course of treatment to give a good chance of lasting success.

The basic idea

The alarm is intended to help the child's body to learn the automatic reactions needed to stay dry at night when this has not happened in the normal course of events. It is an aid to learning. Whatever the reasons may be for a child's lack of skill at bladder control, and whether he or she has never become reliably dry or has started wetting again after a period of dryness, use of the alarm means that there is a good chance that the necessary body learning will take place. Learning bladder control skills with the help of an enuresis alarm does not however necessarily follow the same pattern as the usual learning of control during infancy.

The standard alarm simply produces a loud sound when wetting happens in bed. A loud sound set off as soon as urine begins to be passed will normally produce two reactions. Firstly, the stream of urine stops as the child jumps slightly – this causes the pelvic floor muscles around the urethra (the tube carrying urine from the bladder to the outside of the body) to tighten up, so squeezing the urethra shut. The slight jump and closing off of the urethra is quite automatic; the reader may have noticed that normal urination is shut off briefly if there is a sudden and loud noise while you are in the middle of emptying your bladder. The second reaction is that the child is woken up by the sound of the alarm.

A number of different enuresis alarms are available, but all follow the same basic principles and consist of the same basic elements. The alarm has two main component parts: the first is a urine detector (a special sheet, pad, mat or plate), which is connected by a wire to the rest of the alarm and which sends a signal along the wire to the alarm box when it gets wet; the second is the alarm box, containing a sound unit which makes the necessary noise once the detector has been wetted, together with the battery and necessary electronic circuitry. The early alarms had bells that rang, or buzzers like those also found on people's front doors – hence the names 'bell and pad' or 'buzzer' – but such is progress that the most modern alarms have electronic bleepers and contain the latest in electronic circuitry. **Figure 6** illustrates one widely available type of enuresis alarm, in which the urine detector is a special plastic sheet with metal electrode strips on its surface, which goes under the bottom sheet beneath the child in bed, and

49

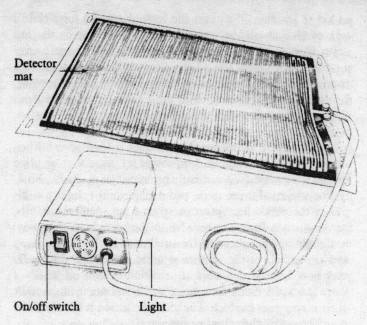

Detector mat

On/off switch   Light

Fig.6 Typical bedwetting alarm (bed type)

the alarm box is placed beside the bed. Another, increasingly popular, type of alarm is a miniature version which is worn on the child's nightclothes, in which the detector is a small plate worn attached to the child's underclothes and the alarm box is attached to the nightdress or pyjama top (see **Figure 9**, see p. 69). Although most children are naturally wary of enuresis alarms because they are unfamiliar bits of equipment, they are generally rather less complicated and less mysterious than any good alarm clock.

How control is learned

The alarm relies on a number of different types of learning in its treatment of bedwetting. The precise blend of these types of learning taking place during treatment is likely to differ from one child to another, and may well alter over the

50

period of one course of treatment of any particular child.

In order to stay dry at night, when the bladder is full and beginning its automatic contractions ready to empty, the child (or adult) needs his or her body to do two things, and to do them in time to prevent the bladder's automatic activities from starting the urine flowing into the bed. The first is to tighten up the muscles of the pelvic floor to keep the outlet tube (urethra) from the bladder firmly and safely closed. The second is to wake up, if still necessary, in time to get safely to the toilet without accidents. Both the 'tightening up' and 'waking up' reactions are important, although different people's bodies tend to rely more on one of the two than the other. Some people usually 'hold on' all night, making especially good use of the 'tightening up' reaction, while others often wake in the night to use the toilet, their bodies mainly using the 'tightening up' response to hold on to the urine while they are waking up and getting to the toilet.

The two vital reactions of 'tightening up' and 'waking up' are precisely the two reactions that the alarm sound usually produces when it goes off; producing tightening up when the body jumps slightly to the sudden sound, and waking the child in exactly the same way as the sound of an alarm clock. Because the alarm goes off each time wetting starts to happen in the bed, alarm treatment makes sure that tightening up and waking up follow the sensations of a full bladder, night after night. Even if a full bladder has not before produced the tightening up and waking up reactions needed to stay dry, the child's body eventually learns to link these reactions to the sensation of a full bladder, because the alarm sees to it that they come together so often. The learning involved in making this link is quite automatic – it cannot be achieved by voluntary effort. If it is slow to happen, or fails to happen at all and alarm treatment does not achieve dryness, it is not through any lack of effort or will to learn by the child. This learning by association is technically known as 'classical conditioning', and is like the one made famous by Pavlov's early experiments with animals. By repeatedly associating food with the sound of a bell, he taught

51

animals to respond automatically with the bodily response of salivation.

The bedwetting child's association between a full bladder on the one hand, and the 'tightening and waking' produced by the alarm on the other hand, grows in strength as treatment progresses, and his or her body begins to produce 'tightening and waking' as its own automatic responses to a full bladder, relying less and less on the alarm to make those responses happen. By the end of a successful course of treatment, one or both of the tightening and waking reactions will begin to occur as the bladder nears its usual 'full' level, but well before wetting begins, so that the former bedwetter either holds his or her urine well enough to last the night without wetting, or wakes in time to visit the toilet.

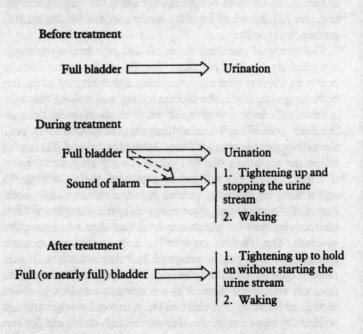

Fig.7 'Classical' learning in bedwetting alarm treatment

Figure 7 summarises the stages of learning by association through alarm treatment in the form of a diagram. The dotted arrow shows the link forged by learning through association during treatment.

Because stopping the stream of urine is involved in alarm treatment, first as a reaction to the noise of the alarm and then as a learned response to a full or nearly full bladder, alarm treatment helps a child to develop the ability to hold on to an increased quantity of urine. Thus use of the alarm tends to increase the bladder's 'functional capacity' – the amount of urine it is prepared to hold before starting to contract ready to empty. Alarm treatment does not therefore only train a child to wake up instead of wetting, as is often supposed, but it also helps to train the bladder to be able to contain more urine for a longer time. For some children, but not all, the alarm enables them to store the entire night's output of urine without either wetting or waking.

Just as people differ in how much their bodies normally use each of the 'holding' and 'waking' skills to stay dry at night, so some children who have been treated with the alarm become good 'holders' and usually sleep the night through, while others will become good 'wakers', waking most nights to use the toilet but learning from the alarm to wake in good time to avoid accidents. Many keep dry with a mixture of holding and waking skills.

Another type of learning involved in alarm treatment is when the body adjusts its reactions according to the consequences. This is technically termed 'operant conditioning'. It is well known (both from common experience and from detailed research work) that an action or reaction, even of an automatic bodily type, will become stronger and more likely to happen again if it is followed by pleasant consequences. An action or reaction which is followed by unpleasant consequences will tend, under certain circumstances, to become weaker and less likely to happen again. Obviously, rewards and punishments work on this principle, but the ways in which the body's automatic functions operate are often moulded or changed by the same principle, and can be altered by quite subtle, less obvious and naturally occurring consequences following any particular bodily action or reaction.

In alarm treatment, the central responses of tightening up and waking up, first to the alarm sound and then, through association, to a full bladder, are strengthened and encouraged because they lead to the pleasant consequences of a dry night and not being woken in a wet bed by a noisy alarm. Wetting triggers a sequence of unwelcome consequences for the body, including a loud noise, disturbed sleep, the discomfort and disappointment of realising that the bed is wet, a trip from bed to the toilet, and the changing of wet sheets and nightclothes. The body will quite naturally tend to adjust its functioning to avoid these consequences of wetting – encouraging it to use its new tightening up and waking responses. The fact that the alarm produces these consequences immediately wetting begins and so immediately after the bodily actions that led to urine beginning to flow inappropriately, makes their effect on body functioning far stronger than the negative consequences of waking up hours later in the morning to find that the bed has been wet at some time in the night. Parents who punish a bedwetter when they find the bed wet will have little or no effect at all on the bedwetting (apart from making the child miserable). This kind of consequence is too remote from the bodily actions that take place at the time of wetting, and which one wants to influence. Only a device like the alarm can act quickly enough (within seconds) to produce consequences likely to affect wetting.

Once tightening up and waking up have been learned from the alarm by association with a full bladder, thus becoming alternatives to wetting when the bladder begins to contract, a full bladder becomes not only the trigger for these two actions, but also a signal to the body that following the 'tightening and waking' chain of events will lead to more pleasant consequences than following the 'automatic wetting' chain of events. There is a great deal of evidence that many of the human body's courses of action are selected in response to this kind of learned signal (known as a 'discriminative stimulus'), which is rather like a signpost signalling what will happen at the end of two alternative courses of action. The fact that a loud sound keeps being added, by the alarm, to the signals coming from a full bladder helps the child's brain, quite automatically, to notice those 'bladder signals' as soon as they begin to come at night.

In discussing the effects of consequences upon bodily actions, it must again be stressed that this process does *not* mean that the child could therefore have exercised any voluntary or conscious control over the actions that can be influenced by consequences. Actions can be changed over a period of time by their associations and consequences where voluntary effort alone has no effect at all. The learning involved is making adjustments to the body's automatic control system; not something that can be achieved by 'trying hard' or remembering. The same types of learning can, in other types of treatment, adjust other quite automatic body functions like heart rate. A child can no more learn 'by trying' to make his body perform the right actions to stay dry at night, than he or she can change his heart rate by willpower alone.

In addition to the types of learning described, it is likely that impressive procedures and confidence that cure is on its way do contribute a lot to the success of treatment in some not fully understood manner. This happens with most treatments, for most types of problem. It is well known that even tablets containing no medication at all, nevertheless often have an effect on medical conditions – an odd phenomenon known as the 'placebo effect'. Treatments are affected by the individual's confidence in them. It seems that a placebo effect adds to the effectiveness of the learning processes involved in alarm treatment – children have even been known to improve with alarms that have broken down, and the likelihood of becoming dry without any actual treatment increases markedly as soon as an appointment to start any form of treatment is arranged. Nearly one in ten children on waiting lists for appointments at bedwetting clinics become dry before their appointment date!

In summary, successful use of an enuresis alarm produces

the responses of muscle tightening to stop urination, and waking; links these to bladder fullness through repeated association of the two; helps the body to notice bladder sensations, and encourages the two necessary responses to happen regularly through their consequences.

The following processes in treatment have been identified:

1. The alarm produces i: tightening of muscles to stop urination and ii: waking, these become increasingly linked to a full bladder and are eventually actually *produced* by a full bladder;
2. These two responses are encouraged and strengthened as an alternative chain of events to bedwetting, because of the very different consequences of each chain of events;
3. The bladder reaching its usual 'full' level becomes i: a trigger for these new responses to happen, eventually without the help of the alarm, and ii: a signal that the tightening up and/or waking chain of events is the one for the body to select in order to secure the more pleasant set of consequences;
4. The bladder adjusts to contain more urine before reaching its 'usual full' level, and therefore 'holds on' longer before beginning its contractions ready to empty;
5. The unexplained 'placebo effect' of confidence in the treatment helps progress towards success.

Effectiveness

The very numerous research studies of enuresis alarm treatment have reported success rates varying between 65 and 100 per cent of those treated. Overall, one may expect a successful outcome with approximately eight out of every ten children or young people treated, assuming that the alarm is used properly. Put another way, every child starting a course of alarm treatment has an eight in ten chance of being dry at the end of it, if the treatment is properly carried out.

Research studies have shown that alarm treatment helps

to produce dry nights much better than simply leaving a child to 'grow out of it' (as was noted in Chapter Three, between 13 and 16 per cent of bedwetters do 'grow out' of the problem in any one year). Research studies comparing alarm treatment with other approaches have shown that the training effect of the alarm, triggered as it is at the moment of wetting, is far greater than alarm clocks or other means of waking a child at night which are not linked to the moment of wetting. Comparisons between the enuresis alarm and other treatments for bedwetting have usually found the alarm to be more effective. It has been found to work better than the 'talking psychotherapy' type of treatment, and has longer-lasting effects for most children than do the various drug treatments.

In speaking of the effectiveness of any form of treatment, it is important to consider how likely it is that the initial cure will last. Therefore, much research has been carried out into 'relapse rates', that is, the likelihood that the child, once dry after treatment, might start to wet the bed again later on. This has been noted already as the major drawback with drug treatments for bedwetting. The relapse rate for basic alarm treatment used to be approximately one in three; thus only two out of every three children initially cured by the alarm could be expected to stay dry for good. This relapse rate was lower than one would expect after drug treatment, but was still disappointingly high. The 'overlearning' technique described in the next chapter, involving extra drinking towards the end of treatment, reduces the chances of relapse by building a 'safety margin' of extra learning into the cure. By adding overlearning to basic alarm treatment, the chances of relapse can be reduced in most cases to just under 13 per cent. In other words, almost 9 out of 10 children cured by alarm treatment with overlearning will remain dry. It is therefore recommended that overlearning should be used wherever possible.

Although it is effective, it is nevertheless true that the enuresis alarm is extremely hard work for parents and child alike. It should not be taken on lightly, but only after careful weighing of the pros and cons within the family. Some people (including some children) do in fact prefer wet beds to alarm treatment – although this view should not be adopted if the bedwetting child himself or herself is distressed by the problem. Both in special enuresis clinics using the alarm, and amongst parents using the alarm privately with their children, as many as one in every three who begin the treatment will give up before it is completed. Giving up happens quickly where there are unexpected practical problems or where progress is not made, and help or guidance is not at hand to help sort out the difficulty. Parents using an alarm obtained privately rather than from the doctor or clinic find it extremely useful to have the advice of someone who has successfully used an alarm before, either as a professional or as a parent.

The most common cause of parents giving up alarm treatment is the failure of the alarm to awaken the child, yet there are ways of dealing with this problem in most cases. These are described later in this book. Failure to wake can in many cases be avoided altogether by ensuring that some very common but simple mistakes are not made in the use of the alarm. As has already been described, waking up is not the be all and end all of alarm treatment; the 'tightening up' response is just as, and for some children more, important. It is however not such an obvious response to the alarm unless you know what to look for, and, disappointingly, many have given up courses of alarm treatment where the child was not waking, without ever realising that this is only one of the responses involved in successful treatment.

Can success or failure be predicted?

It would be very useful indeed if the outcome of a course of treatment could be predicted at the beginning, and much research (including a series of studies by the present writer) has been carried out into the possibility that the alarm may be more or less effective depending on the child's age, sex, or frequency of wet nights. Research findings on the prediction of success have not always agreed on what factors can, and what cannot, predict whether a particular child is likely to become dry on alarm treatment. Some studies have found that failure is more likely where there are serious family or housing problems, but studies disagree over whether wetting that started after a period of dryness, or wetting that is accompanied by daytime urgency or frequency of the need to use the toilet, are more difficult to treat.

Overall, the more obvious factors have not been found to predict the result of alarm treatment for a particular child. Taking children as young as four upwards, the effectiveness of alarm treatment is the same at all ages right through to adulthood; boys and girls have equal chances of success; and 'every night' wetting responds at a similar rate to 'once a week' wetting. Although the treatment involves learning, the outcome of treatment is not affected by the child's intelligence. Physically, the amount of urine the child's bladder is used to holding before it needs emptying does not appear to affect the outcome. Importantly, children who have not responded to alarm or to other forms of treatment in the past, or who have already relapsed to wetting again after an earlier treatment, do no worse with a new course of treatment than those who have never been treated before.

The one factor that research has found to affect and predict the outcome of alarm treatment is that of the attitudes of child and parents towards bedwetting itself. My own research, with a written test I had designed of parents' attitudes towards bedwetting, found that families where the parent is intolerant of bedwetting are significantly more likely than others to give treatment up, and this result has been found by other researchers. Recent research on children's attitudes towards bedwetting has found that children who are worried about their bedwetting, and who see it as being a problem for them socially and emotionally, rather than just giving some practical difficulties, are likely to do better in treatment. In short, a child who worries about bedwetting as a major problem in his or her life can be reassured that he or she stands a good chance of doing well in treatment.

One research study has also recently found that a child who is worried about bedwetting is, if anything, less likely to relapse to wetting after treatment. Again, it is reassuring to know that the child for whom becoming and staying dry matters most stands a better, rather than a worse, chance of becoming dry on treatment, and of staying dry afterwards. Apart from this, relapse to wetting after treatment does not appear to be predictable. Factors such as the child's age, sex, original frequency of wet nights, lifelong wetting before treatment, intelligence, and even whether relapse has happened after treatment in the past, are all unrelated to the chances of staying dry or relapsing after treatment. In one of my own studies, I checked 40 different factors to see if they were possible predictors of relapse. None were. Clearly, a course of treatment without sufficient commitment from the child and the family, or which runs into difficulties which cannot be resolved, will probably not succeed. Stress is known to damage bladder control, and it can both reduce the chances of treatment success, and in some cases trigger renewed wetting by breaking down the all-important learning gained from the alarm.

Apart from these issues, any child or young person starting a course of treatment has the same eight in ten chance as anyone else of success, and any child or young person cured by an alarm plus overlearning has the same risk of slightly over one in ten that they may wet again enough to need a second course of treatment.

FIVE

USING THE ENURESIS ALARM AT HOME

Suitability of the treatment

Treatment of bedwetting with the enuresis alarm may be regarded as the best choice amongst the available range of treatments, provided that its use is practicable in a given situation and provided that enough effort and commitment can be put into using it. It can be used with children from four upwards and is suitable, and equally effective, throughout the school age range. It is also suitable for adults (other than for elderly people). Alarms are not suitable for the early toilet training of very young children (under four years of age), because nerve and muscle systems are not sufficiently developed for the learning involved to take place. The alarm can be used with mentally handicapped children and adults so long as the practicalities of treatment can be coped with, and with people who have a physical handicap so long as medical advice regards it as suitable. Medical confirmation that the alarm is appropriate must be sought before using an alarm with someone, adult or child, who is mentally or physically handicapped, as its use may be inappropriate in certain cases. Alarms are not really suitable for wetting that occurs only occasionally before the start of treatment (less than once a week on average), because such low wetting frequencies do not trigger the alarm often enough to produce a strong learning effect.

Alarms can be used in many circumstances that may seem far from ideal. A single bedroom for the child being treated is a helpful luxury, but is by no means necessary. Most of the writer's patients have used the alarm in shared bedrooms, and some have successfully used alarms in dormitories at school or in children's homes. As described in the last chapter, alarms are equally suitable for boys and girls, even where alarms or other forms of treatment have failed in the past. These failures do not necessarily show that the treatment is unsuitable for the child concerned, but are far more often the result of lack of guidance on how to use the alarm properly, or of practical hitches that parents couldn't resolve at the time.

Medical contact

Parents should always seek a doctor's opinion regarding persistent bedwetting, in case an infection needs attention, and in order to check on the possibility that their child may be one of the very few bedwetters with some other, but connected, physical problem.

Many doctors' practices and child clinics have access to enuresis alarms that can be used in cases they consider to be suitable, in which case this chapter should help by supplementing the information and supervision available from doctor, health visitor or nurse. Naturally, medical opinion on the alarm and other bedwetting treatments varies, and some doctors and clinics prefer other approaches to the problem. In such cases, it is important that parents should discuss the position with their doctor and follow his or her advice with regard to their particular child. The enuresis alarm is a useful treatment for most children, but your doctor is in the best position to judge whether or not this holds true for a particular boy or girl that he or she has examined. Parents obtaining an alarm privately, after receiving a doctor's advice that the alarm is a suitable treatment for their child, should find sufficient guidance in the following sections to see them through the ups and downs of the course of treatment.

A doctor consulted about a child's bedwetting will usually wish to take a urine specimen to check whether the urine is normal or whether there is evidence of an infection, or anything else needing attention. Often, a 'midstream' specimen of urine will be asked for (an 'MSU'), which, as its name implies, is the

62

middle part rather than the first part of the urine passed. The reason for this is that the first part of the stream of urine washes out skin cells and other matter, and therefore gives a less clear picture than the rest of the contents of the bladder. Taking a urine specimen usually means no more than filling a small bottle for the doctor to send off for testing at the laboratory. There, the specimen is examined and, if an infection is found, tests are carried out to find out which antibiotics will combat the infection and so can be recommended to the doctor as a suitable treatment. It is important to tell the child what the urine specimen is for – otherwise it remains just one of those embarrassingly unbelievable things doctors ask us to do!

Doctors consulted about a bedwetting child rarely need to do more than a brief physical examination and take a urine specimen. More complicated checks done at a hospital are usually only arranged where there is good reason to suspect that the problem is more than the straightforward lack of bladder control skills.

Types of alarm apparatus

Figure 6, see p. 50, illustrates a typical 'bed-type' enuresis alarm, made up of an alarm box (containing the device that generates the alarm sound together with the battery and the necessary circuitry), and a urine detector mat connected to the box by a thin flexible cable. The main alternative type of alarm is the miniature 'personally worn' version, with a much smaller alarm box that can be worn on a vest, pyjama jacket or nightdress (instead of placed next to the bed), and a small detector plate that is worn on the front of the child's pants (rather than a larger detector mat that goes under the bottom sheet the child lies on in bed).

A wide variety of alarms is available, and many manufacturers will sell or hire their equipment directly to the public. This may be a way of obtaining an alarm if none are available locally from doctor or clinic. However, apparatus should only be obtained in this way when the child's doctor is in agreement, and approves of the particular type of equipment to be bought, hired or borrowed. This is important, as not all equipment is equally safe or reliable. The Department of Health and Social Security have issued detailed safety specifications for enuresis alarms (specification R/E 1004/03, Issue II, March 1988). It is absolutely essential that any alarm used conforms to the latest version of these specifications. The specifications current at the time of writing this edition of this book are reproduced as an appendix at the back of the book. If you are buying or hiring an alarm privately, check with the manufacturer before you commit yourself that the model you are thinking of purchasing does conform to these specifications (quote the DHSS reference). Home-made or old equipment should never be used. Modern alarms are battery operated, and must not be connected to the electricity mains supply.*

Different sounds are produced by different types of alarm, and there can be quite marked differences in sound even between alarms of the same type. The noisiest alarms are not necessarily the most effective at arousing the bedwetting child: children seem to respond to the alarm which is 'right' for them rather than simply to the loudest. Also, the sound actually reaching the child's ears at night is much affected by the size and furnishing of the bedroom. Extremely loud alarms do produce a somewhat better response, particularly in children making only slow progress with treatment, but they can of course be much more disruptive to use. Common battery-powered bed-type alarms produce a sound in the region of 80 to 90 decibels. Some alarm boxes allow for a choice or adjustment of the alarm sound produced. If such a facility is incorporated, it is worth experimenting with each sound for one to two weeks at a time to discover whether there is one that is more effective for a particular child.

Some bed-type alarms have as an optional extra a plug-

*The writer normally uses Eastleigh MoH or 'Mini-Drinite' apparatus, manufactured by N.H. Eastwood & Son Ltd, 70 Nursery Road, London N14 5QH.

in booster buzzer or vibrator unit. Similarly, there are also vibrator versions of the personally worn types of alarm. These can be very useful where a child does not respond to the sound produced by the standard alarm box, and a unit which emits a low vibrating sound can be particularly effective when placed under the pillow or on the bed-head. Another plug-in optional extra that may be available is an extension buzzer unit with a long enough cable to reach a parents' bedroom or living-room some distance from the child's room. This is useful where parents need to help the child, but do not hear the alarm going off in the child's bedroom. Where such an extension buzzer would be helpful but is not available, a standard type of 'baby intercom' between child's room and parents' bedroom or living-room will serve exactly the same purpose. Many bed-type alarms incorporate a small light which helps to show where the box (and more importantly, its off-switch!) is in the dark.

A number of different designs of urine detector mat or plate are used with different alarms. All these comprise a pair of metal electrodes which trigger the alarm sound in the alarm box when they are connected by urine. In most systems, urine simply serves to connect one electrode to the other, closing an electrical circuit so that a tiny electric current can flow. Urine thus performs the same task that a simple switch would do in the circuit. In an alternative system, the two electrodes are made of different metals which generate a small amount of electricity when they are soaked in urine. This is in turn detected by the electronic circuitry in the alarm box.

The one safety risk with enuresis alarms is that badly designed or wrongly functioning equipment can irritate or damage the child's skin, and early alarm equipment very occasionally caused 'buzzer ulcers'. This problem is avoidable by using good quality modern alarms which conform to current Department of Health and Social Security safety requirements and taking old alarms, whose components may begin to fail, out of use. The cause of the problem is an electric current flowing between two detector electrodes that are both touching the child's skin. The Department of Health and Social Security safety specifications (see the Appendix p. 169) require modern alarms to prevent this problem by the design of the electrical circuits of the alarm limiting the current that can flow across the detector electrodes to safe levels. The specifications even require this limitation to operate safely if the alarm is faulty. It is not however automatic that all alarms available will conform to the specifications, which is why the hirer or purchaser should check that the model that interests them does. As an added precaution, it is important that the detector metal electrodes do not come into direct contact with the child's skin. Skin irritation is extremely unlikely to be a problem when using safe alarms properly. I have only ever come across one child with a sore caused by an enuresis alarm, despite treating a very great number of children for bedwetting since 1971. The problem is raised here because it is the main risk that would be run by using home-made equipment, or old equipment without the modern protective circuitry and not conforming with the latest safety requirements.

Alarms can be put into four main categories, whose advantages and disadvantages are as follows:

1. *Bed-type alarm with twin detector mats*
This is the original type of enuresis alarm, with an alarm box that goes next to the child's bed, and a detector system that goes in the bed underneath the bottom sheet. The detector system has two mats made either of fine wire mesh or metal foil, which go into the bed one on top of the other with a layer of bed sheet between them, to form a 'sandwich'. The two mats may be of different metals in the 'electricity generating' type of detector system. Metal foil mats usually use an upper foil with holes through it (so that urine can pass through) and a lower foil without holes. Twin mat arrangements are robust and particularly safe in use (it is very difficult for both electrodes to touch the child at the same time) and many children prefer the traditional bed-type of alarm to the newer personally worn type because nothing is attached to them. It is necessary,

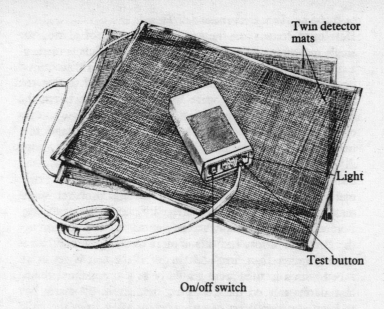

Twin detector mats

Light

Test button

On/off switch

Fig.8 Bedwetting alarm with twin bed mats

however, for the child to sleep naked below the waist, to allow urine to soak the detector mats quickly (rather than soaking into nightclothes first), and this is something that matters to some children.

Bed-type alarms have a good-sized alarm box, with controls that are simple for both parent and child to operate and easy to find at night, and with scope for plug-in optional extras like booster buzzers, vibrator units for children who do not 'tighten up' and/or wake up to the alarm sound alone, and extension buzzers. The disadvantages of the twin mat alarm are that an extra layer of bed sheet (or a pillowcase) is needed, unlike other types of alarm. This adds to the washing to be done until the child is dry, and making the bed up with two detector mats is slightly more complicated than making it up with only one. **Figure 8** illustrates a standard type of twin mat, bed-type alarm.

2. Bed-type alarm with single detector mat

Developed from the original twin mat type of alarm, the single mat alarm uses only one detector mat. This is made of a plastic material with both the metal detector electrodes on its surface in a pattern of metal strips, arranged so that the alarm is triggered when urine 'bridges the gap' between the electrode strips. The single mat alarm has all the advantages of being a bed-type of alarm, with the added advantages that its single mat is easier to make up in the bed, easier to wipe dry (particularly useful in the middle of the night!), and doesn't need the extra layer of sheet required with the twin mat arrangement, thus saving on the washing. However, single mats are rather more easily damaged by heavy use or misuse. Folding, creasing or scratches on the mat surface can damage the electrode strips, and this is more likely if the mattress is sagging rather than firm and flat, or if the mat is set up in a bed which is then used regularly as a trampoline! Single mat alarms rely on the electronic circuitry in the alarm box to keep any significant electric current away from the child should he or she lie with both electrodes touching the skin (this is more likely to happen with a single mat alarm than a twin mat one). It is therefore extremely important that one uses the modern alarms of this type which have the necessary protective circuitry in them, and not old and obsolete equipment which may not have the necessary protective electronics. **Figure 6**, see p. 50; illustrates a modern single mat bed-type alarm.

3. Personally worn alarm

The personally worn alarm is small and worn on the child's nightclothes, as an alternative to lying on the detector with a box next to the bed. The personally worn alarm is much preferred by some children and young people. Having the alarm sound that much nearer to the child means that it does not have to be quite so noisy, and this can be an advantage in some homes. Also, and this matters a lot to some children and young people, is that one does not need to sleep naked below the waist.

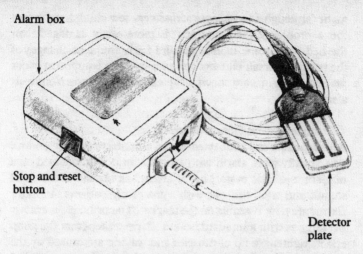

Alarm box

Stop and reset button

Detector plate

Fig.9 A typical personally worn bedwetting alarm

Because the detector plate is worn against the front of the child's pants, it gets wet more rapidly than a detector mat in the bed would as it is closer to the source of the urine. The alarm sound is therefore triggered more quickly and the child's body may 'tighten up' and stop the urine stream more quickly than with a bed-type alarm. This should encourage treatment progress, and can mean less urine in the bed on wet nights, particularly in the later stages of treatment. Research has shown that personally worn alarms will get the same number of children dry as bed alarms, but that they can be expected to get children dry quicker. The night clothing worn by the child also soaks up some of the urine on wet nights, which would otherwise soak into the bed. At the beginning of treatment this will not save the bedding, but when the amount of urine on wet nights becomes quite small later on in treatment, it can mean wet clothing but dry bedding – and wet nightclothes are easier to change at night and to wash in the morning, than wet sheets. Disadvantages of personally worn alarms are that the alarm box can be uncomfortable for some children because they cannot find a good position without lying on it during the

69

night (although I have come across very few children who find this a problem); the equipment is more easily damaged than the bed-type; some models require fairly frequent changes of the relatively small battery; and plug-in extra equipment is not practicable. **Figure 9** shows a typical personally worn enuresis alarm.

4. *Personally worn vibrator alarm*
A few years ago I requested alarm manufacturers to produce a personally worn alarm with a small vibrator unit (based on a miniature electric motor) in the alarm box instead of the usual sound, and tried this out with some of my patients. Vibrator alarms are now available on the market. The principle is exactly the same as with a standard 'sound' alarm, except that the jump effect, tightening up of muscles and waking are caused by the vibration suddenly starting instead of by a sudden noise. The advantages of this are that the alarm can be used without disturbing anyone else, and that the vibration often produces a response in those who have failed to respond to 'sound' alarms, including children with hearing problems. The vibrator alarm is therefore well worth trying where response to standard alarm treatment has been disappointing (particularly if the child's body did not 'tighten up' and wake up to alarm sounds). A vibrator will, of course, only be effective if the child or young person does tighten up and/or wake up to the vibration, and this needs checking at the beginning. The vibrator alarm, being much more 'private' than alarms that make a noise, is preferred by many older children, teenagers and adults, and those needing to use alarm treatment in places like boarding schools or student hostels. The disadvantage is that no one else can help the child to wake to the alarm, because no one else will hear it. If a child or young person's body does respond to the vibration, and he or she can cope alone with changing clothing and bedding, then the vibrator allows the child to treat him or her self for bedwetting without disturbing or involving anyone else, and this can be important – for instance, if parents have real need of undisturbed sleep, or have problems staying

tolerant of the child when he triggers a sound alarm. Apart from its use of vibration, the vibrator alarm shares the other pros and cons of sound-type personally worn alarms.

Manufacturers are continuing development work on alarms, and the future range of alarms looks likely to include other designs, such as alarms using radio signals instead of wires, alarms that can trigger a range of other equipment (like radio or tape recorder) to wake the child, and even an alarm that replays a pre-recorded waking message from the child himself!

Before starting treatment – setting up the progress record

At least two weeks (and preferably four weeks) before starting alarm treatment, it is important to stop any other special procedures or treatments being used for bedwetting (checking that this is in order with the doctor before stopping any treatments that he or she has prescribed), and to start keeping a simple record of wet and dry nights. By doing this, a 'baseline' record of the child's own bladder control can be obtained, against which you can later measure progress on the alarm. If you do not have a record of what wetting was like before starting treatment, then it is extremely difficult to judge how much effect the treatment is having. Wetting frequencies shown on record charts often differ a great deal from one's general estimates of how often wetting is happening, and therefore it is only with an accurate 'baseline' record before treatment began that one can properly assess how much progress is being made (or whether progress is not being made) during treatment.

Figure 10 shows a simple wet and dry record chart which is suitable for keeping a record both before and during alarm treatment. The chart for some children will simply show every night wet, but for many the wetting pattern will be very irregular. An irregular pattern is quite normal, and one should avoid the temptation to look for reasons to explain why one night was wet and another one dry. With any poorly developed skill, including poor bladder control, successes and accidents will tend to be mixed together more or less at ran-

71

Night record sheet
Please check whether the bed is wet or dry each morning   Put 'W' for wet, 'D' if dry

	Week 1	Week 2	Week 3	Week 4	Week 5	Week 6	Week 7	Week 8	Week 9	Week 10	Week 11	Week 12
Monday												
Tuesday												
Wednesday												
Thursday												
Friday												
Saturday												
Sunday												

Fig.10   Simple wet/dry chart

dom. The bedwetter will wet frequently and unpredictably, for no special reason other than the fact that he or she is not yet very good at bladder control, just as the toddler learning to walk will frequently fall down for no reason other than the fact that he is not yet very skilful at walking. In both cases, an appropriate record chart would show a thinner 'scatter' of accidents as the skill improves.

In a very few cases indeed, there may be some real pattern to wetting which is likely to show up on a chart, and which may continue to show up during treatment. Some patterns are fairly common and mean little – many children's wetting is slightly worse in colder weather or if they are unwell or anxious about something. Some children's wetting varies between school term-time and holiday periods – this may be nothing more than the common variations in wetting between different circumstances, and does not necessarily mean that anything is wrong either at school or at home. However, a clear pattern, particularly one that carries on during treatment, does suggest a check to see whether there is some source of stress the child would be better without. If it is possible to relieve such pressure (and it may well not be possible), the removal of stress is likely to help the child to learn bladder control more quickly from the enuresis alarm. Even so, patterns in a child's wetting that appear on a chart commonly disappear as treatment continues, and have no real significance at all.

Because of the usually random pattern of wetting, it is helpful to keep a score of wet nights out of seven each week, and to plot the weekly scores on a straightforward graph. The graph in **Figure 15**, see p. 98, shows the weekly scores of wet nights for one of my own patients plotted in this way, making it very easy to see how the child's bedwetting is changing over the weeks as she responds to alarm treatment. The weekly scores, and thus the graph, will vary up and down quite markedly for many children, but the overall level and trend in wetting (and in becoming dry) can usually be seen quite clearly. Even during successful treatment, wetting will still tend to happen fairly randomly, and a short run of wet nights after a good run of dry nights does not mean disaster. This happened more than once with my patient shown, as the graph in **Figure 15** shows: it is the trend over a period of time that needs to be looked for.

It is very useful if the child can keep his or her own record chart and fill it in, under supervision as necessary. An older child or young person can usually take charge of the record-keeping. It is not unknown for a child involved in recording his or her own wetting to improve markedly even before treatment begins. At one of my special bedwetting treatment clinics, almost one in ten children became dry in this way alone!

If the child has other problems of bladder control, it is useful for some simple record of these to be kept as well. Another chart can be used if daytime wetting is a problem, to keep a record of wet and dry days. This will show whether, as often happens, daytime wetting is reducing in line with any reductions in night-time wetting produced by the alarm. If urgency to empty the bladder during the day is a problem, or if the child needs to go to the toilet to urinate much more often than most other children, a record can be kept of these problems by noting each week whether the problem was 'high' 'medium' or 'low', and adding this rating as an 'H', 'M' or 'L' under each week's records of wets and dries on the chart. Reductions in daytime wetting (known in the jargon as 'diurnal enuresis'), urgency to urinate or frequency in needing to empty the bladder, where any of these are a problem, can be useful early signs that a treatment is having an effect on bladder control.

It is extremely important that the 'W' and 'D' record chart *is* kept going throughout alarm treatment. As has already been underlined, it is the only way progress can be measured with any accuracy, and both parents' and children's own estimates of changes in wetting during treatment are often quite, and surprisingly, different from what is actually happening. At special clinics, I have often come across families where gradual improvements have gone completely unnoticed until

Name _____

Please fill this record in every morning

Record commencing _____

Morning	Was the bed wet (put 'W') or dry (put 'D')?	Did the child wake on his own (without being woken) to use the toilet?	Fill in these details if the alarm went off			
			What time (or times) of night did the alarm go off?	Did the alarm wake the child without anyone else helping?	Size of wet patch – put 'S' for small, 'M' for medium, 'L' for large	Did the child have 'more to do' in the toilet? Put 'S' for small amount, 'M' for medium amount, 'L' for large amount
Saturday						
Sunday						
Monday						
Tuesday						
Wednesday						
Thursday						
Friday						
Saturday						
Sunday						
Monday						
Tuesday						
Wednesday						
Thursday						
Friday						

Fig.11 Detailed treatment record chart

the records are checked, and worse, families convinced that all is well, whose records nevertheless show long periods of no improvement that indicate the need to review treatment procedures. These trends can be seen easily as soon as the weekly wet and dry scores are put onto a graph. The chart encourages the child if progress is shown, and highlights the need to review treatment procedures and perhaps seek advice if it is not. Records do not need to be complicated, but they must be kept up. All that is necessary is to continue to fill in a 'W' or 'D' every morning while the alarm is in use, and, ideally, to add up the total each weekend and put the week's score onto a graph on an ordinary piece of squared paper to show the overall trend.

For a younger child, it is helpful to turn the record chart into the sort of star chart described in Chapter Three, with a stick-on star (or any other easily bought stick-on symbol) put on the chart by the child to celebrate each dry night. If stick-on symbols are not easily available, the child can colour or draw something in the square on the chart instead. As an added encouragement, every so many dries can earn a *small* prize or celebration while treatment is in progress.

If treatment is not progressing well and the situation needs to be reviewed to highlight what the problems might be or monitor the effectiveness of steps being taken to put them right (as described in Chapter Six), then a more detailed record of exactly how the child's body is responding to the alarm can be kept until treatment is again progressing well. A detailed record chart for this purpose is given in **Figure 11**. An older alarm user, or parents wishing to spot signs of progress or problems very early (perhaps because of earlier failure to become dry with an alarm or another form of treatment) may wish to use the more detailed chart throughout treatment instead of the more usual (and easier to keep) 'W and D' chart.

Practical considerations before treatment

Stresses

As has been described, stress or major (but not necessarily stressful) changes in a child's life may have been a factor preventing the sound learning of bladder control at the usual time for some children, or disrupting bladder control (which may already have been shaky in the first place) for others – but any stresses may well have passed and been long forgotten.

Whether a child has always wet the bed, or has become wet again after a period of dryness, and whether stress may have been a factor in the child's body failing to learn bladder control at night in the first place, or in him or her losing it again later, serious stresses at the time of treatment are not helpful. A continuing stress can make learning bladder control more difficult (just as it will make other types of learning more difficult), and it is worth considering before embarking on alarm treatment whether the child or young person is subject to any such major stresses at the time. If nothing immediately springs to mind, no deeper hunting is necessary. If a stress is easily identified, consider whether it is possible to remove or reduce it. If the stress is only temporary, consider whether it would not be better to wait until it is over before starting alarm treatment. The child will be better off without the stress if it can be sorted out, and the effects of treatment are also likely to be more successful without it.

Where a known stress cannot be relieved – perhaps there are family difficulties or continuing problems at school – alarm treatment can still be used effectively, but as it will have one more obstacle to overcome it will need more care, patience and probably persistence than if everything else is going well. It will be particularly important to make sure that the alarm does not have to cope with unresolved treatment problems as well as the stresses. Be prepared to sort out any treatment problems as they occur (see the next chapter), and as necessary to use the more detailed chart given in **Figure 11** on p. 75 to pinpoint any problems and monitor the effectiveness of solutions.

77

There is no reason why an alarm cannot be used effectively with a child or young person who has other psychological problems or major difficulties – these often do not even hinder progress, and if the bedwetting is successfully treated, the other problems are not likely to be affected either positively or negatively. At least the child will end up with one problem less.

Previous experience of treatment

A child's chances of success are not affected by past failures at alarm treatment, or other forms of bedwetting treatment, nor in cases where the child has 'relapsed' to wetting again after an initial success with previous treatment. Because alarm treatment is, sadly, often carried out with little practical guidance or supervision from professionals, many bedwetting children have already experienced an earlier failure with alarm treatment. It is important to know that this does *not* spoil the child's chances of success with a new, properly carried out, course of alarm treatment.

Any problems that were met with in a previous treatment should be noted and a solution worked out or advice sought before trying again. There is nothing so demoralising than meeting the same difficulties a second time around and still not knowing what to do about them. The guidance in this book is intended to cover most of the difficulties people come across in using alarms, but if you have previously experienced a problem that is not covered, seek advice from someone with successful professional experience of using enuresis alarms. Your doctor or the community health offices of the local health authority should be able to put you in touch with an appropriate person.

Sleeping arrangements

Two-thirds of the children treated by the writer with alarms have used them in shared bedrooms. The usual pattern is that when the alarm is first used, others are awoken by it; but they soon become used to it and usually hardly stir at all when the alarm goes off. It is rather like sleeping in a room near a noisy road or railway line – at first, one is disturbed a great deal by the sound, but eventually one adjusts to and hardly notices it. The alarm user and the parent who helps him or her at night do not make this adjustment as they respond to each alarm triggering with a definite routine. Shared bedrooms can be a positive asset where a child has difficulty in waking to the alarm, as a brother or sister can often help to overcome this problem (there are extra procedures to help if a child does not awake to the alarm, given in the next chapter, see p. 107.

Many people using a standard 'sound type' of alarm in the family are concerned at the possibility of the noise disturbing neighbours. While this is not impossible, it is amazing how much sound is absorbed by walls. A more common problem is the parent in another bedroom in the same house failing to hear the alarm!

Where for any reason it is important to avoid waking people other than the alarm user, a personally worn alarm is often the answer. Personally worn 'sound type' alarms are often quieter than the more standard 'beside the bed' alarm box, and if it is essential to avoid a sound, then a personally worn vibrator type alarm is the answer, so long as the alarm user himself or herself is woken by it. The only sound made by a personally worn vibrator alarm is a very slight, low, whirring sound made by the miniature motor inside which causes the vibration, which is not enough sound to carry any distance or disturb anyone else.

Bedding and clothing

Extra bedclothing and extra nightclothes are required when using some types of alarm. With any alarm, the fact that the alarm will wake the child every time he or she wets will make it necessary to provide more changes of bedsheets and pyjamas or pants than before treatment if the child wets more than once during the night. Using a bed-type alarm with two detector mats will require one extra layer of bed linen to go between the two mats: an extra sheet or pillowcase, or a drawsheet. A boy or girl using a personally worn alarm will need to wear two pairs of pants each night. In addition, using a personally worn alarm means the alarm box will be attached to the pyjama jacket or nightdress, ideally by means of a piece of 'Velcro' sewn to the material. Bed-type alarms with a single detector mat are the most economical on washing, as they do not require either any extra bedding or any adaptations to clothing. With any alarm, if treatment is proving successful, the washing of bedding and clothing will reduce as the alarm begins to produce fewer wet nights.

It is important that bed sheets while any type of enuresis alarm is in use should not be made of nylon, even though it is easy to wash. Nylon tends to encourage perspiration, which in turn causes problems by triggering the alarm when the bed and clothing are otherwise dry. For the same reason, nylon pyjamas or nightdresses should not be worn, and nylon pants should not be worn with personally worn alarms. A further problem caused by nylon sheets or pants is that the material does not allow urine to pass through easily, so that if urine has to pass through a layer of nylon before reaching the detector, it will not soak through quickly enough to trigger the alarm rapidly at the start of wetting, something which is necessary to effective treatment.

If a child is too hot in bed and so perspires a great deal, any type of alarm will be set off by perspiration when the child has not wet – the alarm that can tell the difference between urine and perspiration has yet to be invented! It is therefore worth checking that the bedroom is not overheated, and that there is not an excessive amount of bedding on the bed. Continental quilts or duvets often cause problems by making the child hotter in bed than when sleeping under blankets, and it is best not to use a continental quilt while the child is on an alarm to reduce the risk of irritating false alarms caused by perspiration.

More than one bedwetter to be treated in the family
Where more than one child in the family wets the bed, only one at a time should be treated with an alarm. The only

exception is if a vibrator alarm is to be used; although even
then it is unwise to treat more than one child simultaneously
if it is not essential: there will be problems if the vibrator
alarm does not produce the necessary responses and has to be
swopped for a sound-type of alarm. Two sound-type alarms in
the same house can cause chaos! The choice as to who should
be treated first is for the family to make, but preference may
perhaps be given to the child most distressed about, or whose
activities are likely to be the most restricted by bedwetting,
or, these factors being equal, the oldest child.

Explaining to the child

It is extremely important that the child should have the
problem of bedwetting, the use of the alarm, and the way it
is to go about teaching his or her body what to do to stay dry,
explained carefully and in terms that he or she can understand.
The alarm can be a frightening piece of equipment (even if it is
rather less remarkable a device than the average modern alarm
clock), and reassurance is needed that its wires are not going
to be attached to the child himself, that he or she is not going
to have an electric shock, and that the whole thing is basically
simple and friendly. Very few children are frightened by the
alarm if they are properly acquainted with it in the first place.
All children appreciate, and deserve, a sensible explanation of
what it does and how it is intended to help their bodies to
become dry.

In explaining bedwetting to a child, it is helpful to point
out that all children find their bodies are good at some things
and poor at others. Some are good footballers or swimmers or
gymnasts, others are not very good at these things. In the same
way, some are good at controlling their bladders, others not
very good – and that can run in the family. Children whose
bodies find bladder control a problem are not immature, disturbed, odd or peculiar, any more than children who are no
good at football or swimming (or adults who take a long time
to pass their driving tests). I find it helpful to tell my patients
that at school I was hopeless at football, and that they are no

more peculiar because their bodies and brains have problems controlling the bladder than I was (or still am!) because mine has problems in playing football. Being not very good at controlling one's bladder *matters* more, but is just as common as being not very good at some sport or another. In either case, special coaching can improve matters, and this is where the alarm comes in.

The way the alarm helps can be explained to a child along the lines of the following, adapted according to age:

You can move some of the muscles in your body whenever you want to, like raising your arm in the air by using the muscles in your arm. Some other muscles work automatically and you cannot make them do what you want them to do, however hard you try. One muscle like that is the muscle that your heart is made of; it beats on its own, and you can't make it go faster or slower just by trying to. The tank inside you, called your bladder, is made of muscle that works automatically, too. Your bladder works on its own, and even if it works in a way that makes you wet in bed, you cannot change that just by trying hard. The alarm is going to try to teach your body what it has got to do to keep you dry at night, so that afterwards your body will do it automatically – just as it makes your heart work automatically.

When you have a wet night, what happens is that your bladder gets full and sends a message to your brain saying that it needs to be emptied. Your brain, though, is too sleepy to take any notice on most nights – a bit like a radio set that is not quite tuned in, the message might get through every now and again, but it is often not heard at all. When the message does not get through, your bladder just has to empty in your bed and you have a wet night.

When you are using the alarm, the sound (or vibration, if a vibrator alarm is being used) makes you jump a bit. This makes the muscles between your legs tighten up and stop the wee coming out. Then the noise of the alarm wakes you

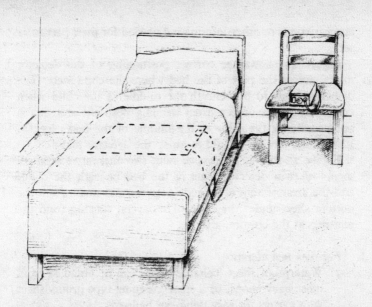

Fig.12 Positioning the béd-type alarm. Note detector mat(s) across the bed, alarm far enough away to need the child to get up to reach it, and cable positioned where it will not be tripped over

up. After a few weeks, your brain gets so used to you stopping weeing and being woken up just after it gets that message saying that your bladder is full, that instead of staying sleepy, it learns to listen to the messages from your bladder, and either wakes you up in time to go to the toilet or tells your body to hold on for a while.

Setting up the apparatus

Bed-type alarms
Different makes of equipment need slightly different procedures, but the guidance in this section will be appropriate to most bed-type alarms using either twin detector mats or a single mat detector system. The maker's instructions will give

83

any variations or other information needed for their particular set.

Figure 12 shows the correct positioning of the detector mat(s) across the part of the bed where the child wets. The detector needs to be beneath the middle of the child when curled up in his or her usual sleeping position, and this is not necessarily the same as the middle of the bed's length. It is in fact rare for a child to 'miss' the detector mat(s).

Figure 13 shows, in cross section, two alternative arrangements of twin detector mats in the bed beneath the child, and the arrangement of a single detector mat underneath the bottom sheet under the child. The layers, starting from the mattress at the bottom, are:

For twin mat alarms:

1. Waterproof sheet (suitable sheets can be obtained from most baby shops, or a small camping-type groundsheet with eyelets for easy tying can be used).

2. First detector mat. With alarms using wire mesh mats, even if these are of two different colours of metal (the different metals used in the 'generating' rather than 'bridging the gap' electrode system) it does not matter which one goes on the bed first. With equipment using mats made of metal foil, the one without holes goes on the bed first.

3. Separating sheet (not made of nylon). This is to keep the mats above and below from actually touching one another. If they do touch, this will not cause any harm, but alarms using the 'bridging the gap' electrode systems will immediately go off, while those using the 'generating' principle will not go off even if the child then wets. To perform its task, the separating sheet should not be torn or threadbare, but it need not cover the whole bed as long as it is big enough to keep the mats apart with a tuck at the sides and a good 'border' around the mats so that they will not touch when the child moves about in the night. A half-sheet or cot-sheet will do. An alter-

84

native (see **Figure 13(b)** is to put the lower detector mat *inside* a pillowcase (not made of nylon), thus dispensing with the need for a separating sheet.

4. Second detector mat, positioned on top of the separating sheet or pillowcase, directly above the lower mat. The connecting terminal needs to be on the same side of the bed as that of the first mat, and for the sake of comfort the two terminals should not be directly on top of one another (this can be avoided by turning the mat the other way up).

5. Bed sheet (again, not made of nylon). This covers the mat arrangement, and is the bottom sheet on which the child lies in the usual way. Although the child will be able to feel the detector mats underneath the sheet, children do not usually find them particularly uncomfortable.

For single mat alarms:

The bed arrangement for single mat alarms is shown in cross section in **Figure 13(c)**. The layers, starting from the mattress upwards, are:

1. Waterproof sheet as above.

2. Detector mat, placed with the foil strip electrodes uppermost where they will be reached by the urine.

3. Bed sheet, not made of nylon. As above, this is the bottom sheet on which the child lies. It is especially important that this sheet covers the detector mat completely, is tucked in well, and does not have threadbare patches or holes in it, as it is important to ensure that the electrode surface does not touch the child's skin.

The leads to the bedside alarm box should be connected to the mats according to the manufacturer's instructions: most alarms use some form of snap connector. If possible, the leads may be left permanently connected to the mats to avoid wear and tear on the connectors, which are relatively weak parts of the detector mats. The alarm box should be placed on a table or chair, or on the floor by the child's bed – positioned so that he or she will not trip over the lead, and put far enough away

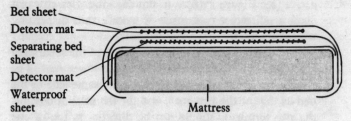

Fig.13a   Section of twin mat arrangement in the bed

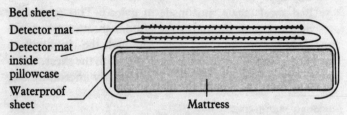

Fig.13b   Section of alternative twin mat arrangement using a pillowcase

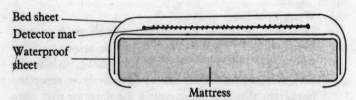

Fig.13c   Section of single mat arrangement in the bed

to require him to rise from the bed to switch it off.

It is helpful if the bed is made up with the alarm well before bedtime on the first night of treatment. If one can spare the sheets, any fears the child might have (or the curiosity of an older child as to how it all works) can be met by a practice triggering of the alarm. To do this, set up and switch on the alarm, then pour a small quantity of water with some salt dissolved in it onto the sheet over the detector mat. (Although many alarms will trigger with fresh water, some need salty water to simulate the properties of urine, and most trigger more quickly than with fresh water). Put firm hand pressure onto the wet patch for a few seconds to simulate the weight of the child sleeping on the sheet, until the water soaks through and wets the detector sufficiently to trigger the alarm. It takes quite a while for the water to soak through and do this: if you are like most people trying it for the first time, you will for a moment think that you are using a dud alarm, then be taken by surprise when it goes off! This delay should be as short as possible when the child is wetting at night, and having tried the alarm you will appreciate that a nylon sheet preventing urine soaking through, or a child wearing nightclothes below the waist which soak up much of the urine, would make the delay unacceptably long. One may wonder why alarms are not made more sensitive, so that less urine on the electrodes would trigger the sound. While this would certainly reduce the delay, it would also increase the number of times the alarm went off because the child was perspiring slightly.

Personally worn alarms

The alarm box needs to be attached to the child's pyjama jacket or nightdress, firmly enough not to fall off at night as the child moves about, easily reached to switch off when it is triggered and one is still quite sleepy, and positioned so that it will not be uncomfortable and always getting laid on. The best position for most children is on the front of the pyjama jacket or nightdress, on one side over the soft part of the shoulder (between the shoulder bone and the collar bone), so that the child will not be too uncomfortable if he or she lies on it. The box can be put into the pocket if there is one, provided that the hole that the sound comes from is pointing upwards, so the sound doesn't get 'lost' inside the pocket, and provided that it doesn't get pulled out by accident each night! If the box tends to hang too loosely on a rather floppy pyjama jacket or nightdress fix it on a vest or T-shirt instead. A top that is getting a bit too small will hold the box especially closely in place. An alternative way of wearing the box is on a wrist strap, usually fixed with Velcro.

Different alarms use different methods of holding the alarm box in place. The best is Velcro, with one patch of the material on the back of the alarm box and the other sewn onto the nightclothes in the appropriate position. This holds the box firmly enough for most children, but allows its easy removal. The disadvantage, of course, is that you have to sew on the strips of material. Some alarms use a safety pin (of the nappy pin type) to hold the box. This is quite effective, but it is preferable to avoid pins if possible in case they come undone (it is of course possible to replace the pin arrangement with a glued Velcro strip on the back of the alarm box).

Sound-type personally worn alarms should be worn on the *outside* of the pyjama jacket or nightdress (or in the chest pocket).

Vibrating-type personally worn alarms should be worn on the *inside* of the pyjama jacket or nightdress, against the collar bone so that the vibration can be felt easily. Some children may find a vest or T-shirt better than a pyjama jacket or nightdress for holding the vibrator alarm box in place against the collarbone. Alternative positions for a vibrating type of alarm box are on a wrist strap against the bony part of the wrist, or on a similar strap against the ankle. Suitable straps can be made up using Velcro to do them up.

The wire connecting the alarm box to the detector plate should be run *outside* the child's pants but *inside* the pyjamas or nightdress, so that the wire is not so easily caught and pulled as the child moves about. This arrangement also makes sure that the alarm box does not accidentally fall down the toilet if it gets pulled off when the child visits the toilet after an alarm triggering!

The detector plate is worn in the same way for boys and girls. It is important that the plate itself should not rest against the skin at night, as this could irritate the skin. The child should put on one pair of pants (not nylon), and the plate should be stuck on the outside of these pants, at the front where it will get wet, with a piece of sticky tape or sticking plaster. Put the tape or plaster across the plastic part of the plate (or the connecting wire if there is not space to do this), to avoid damaging the metal strips on the plate. Then put on a second pair of pants (again, not nylon) on the top so that the plate is now sandwiched between the two pairs of pants. This ensures that the plate is unlikely to get knocked off when the child turns over in bed, and that as soon as wetting begins, the plate will be surrounded by wet material on both sides so that it triggers the alarm quickly.

Briefs are the best type of pants for boys to use with a detector plate. Y-fronts can be used, but are not so good because the pouch part has more than one layer of material for the urine to soak through, and because special care has to be taken in positioning the detector plate over the pouch but well away from the opening so that the boy's penis cannot rest against the plate if it is through the opening at the front of the pants. If you have both briefs and Y-fronts, put the briefs on first, against the skin, and use the Y-fronts as the second pair of pants on top. Boxer shorts are not very suitable, as they are usually too loose to hold the detector plate properly in place.

Some manufacturers of personally worn alarms suggest that the detector plate should be worn fitted inside a small stick-on type of sanitary pad. This is not necessary if the method just described is followed, and using a sanitary pad has the disadvantage that it will slow down the alarm triggering by absorbing urine before it reaches the detector plate – when it is the quick triggering that is the major advantage of the personally worn alarm. The pad absorbing urine before it can reach the detector plate is a particular problem with boys, because the pad does not always get the 'direct hit' with urine that it needs for it to soak quickly to the detector plate inside – and of course, boys are often not keen to wear a sanitary pad once they realise what it is!

Figure 14 illustrates the usual location of the alarm box and the detector plate for personally worn alarms. Note that the wire from the alarm box should run from the box *inside* the

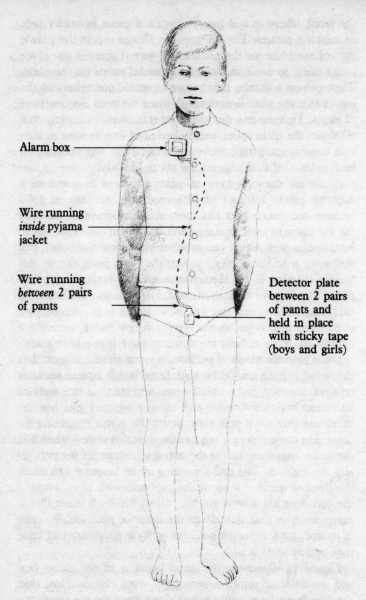

Alarm box

Wire running *inside* pyjama jacket

Wire running *between* 2 pairs of pants

Detector plate between 2 pairs of pants and held in place with sticky tape (boys and girls)

Fig.14 Wearing a personally-worn type of alarm

90

pyjama jacket or nightdress, and then *between* the two pairs of pants to the detector plate.

It is not necessary to wear pyjama trousers or a long nightdress as well as the pants needed with the personally worn alarm, but the child may do so if he or she wishes as long as the extra nightclothing involved does not cause the child to perspire enough to set off the alarm.

It is helpful to spend some time on the first night of alarm use practicing setting it up and finding the right position for everything. It is also important in the morning after the first few nights of use to check whether the positioning and methods used for attaching box and plate were satisfactory, or need amendment. It is worthwhile arranging to start using the alarm at a weekend or in the school holidays so that there is time for this without the usual before-school morning rush.

With either type of alarm, as well as demonstrating what the child needs to do, parents should encourage a young or nervous child to play with the alarm until it is a familiar and no longer a frightening object. Misuse or the dismantling of the alarm is not exactly to be encouraged, but many younger children whose response on first seeing their alarm was tearful have happily gone to bed with it after half an hour pretending its sound is a police siren! A practice triggering of the alarm, with salt water for a bed-type alarm, or by touching the detector plate with a wet finger for a personally worn alarm, is also useful to test the proper operation of the alarm before use, and to make sure that everything is connected up properly.

Nightly routine

Bed-type alarms
While using a bed-type of alarm, the child should sleep without wearing anything below the waist – no pyjama trousers, pants or long nightdresses, to avoid clothing soaking up much of the urine before it can reach the detector mat, so delaying the sounding of the alarm. This sort of delay can seriously reduce the effectiveness of treatment.

If a child is too embarrassed to sleep naked below the waist, even with a dressing-gown ready to grab before leaving the bed, *thin* pyjama trousers or pants (not made of nylon) may be tried as a last resort – but not if there are problems in waking to the alarm, and accepting that the child's response to treatment may be slowed down.

When using a bed-type alarm, wet sheets should be washed before re-use and not simply dried out over a radiator or elsewhere, even if the wet patch was small. This is important because the dried salty residue in the sheets will mean the alarm is easily triggered by perspiration, making disruptive false alarms more likely. Sheets that have become damp enough with perspiration to trigger the alarm should also be washed before re-use, for the same reason.

Each morning, it is important that the detector mat(s) on the bed are carefully flattened out again if they have become crumpled or folded in the night. If this is not done, folds and creases will develop in the detector which will be uncomfortable, and which will shorten the life of the detector. This is easily done by lying each mat on a hard surface (such as a hard floor) and pressing down on folds and crumpled areas.

All types of alarm
The alarm should be used every night, only being left off if there are exceptional reasons for doing so (perhaps when visitors are sleeping in the house, if the child is sleeping away from home, or if the child is ill). A record chart of the simple 'Wet and Dry' type should be used throughout treatment and filled in (ideally by the child if possible) every morning so that treatment progress can be monitored, or the possible lack of it spotted more accurately than is possible without a proper record.

When the alarm goes off at night, the child must:

1. Switch the alarm off as quickly as he or she can. Bedside alarm boxes have a switch on the front. Personally worn alarms have a stop button on the box, and usually need

the detector plate to be taken off the pants and dried before the alarm will stay off.

2. Visit the toilet. Finish emptying the bladder there, or use a pot or bucket in the bedroom if the toilet is a long distance away.

3. Help remake the bed and change out of wet clothes. Parents should help the child as needs be, and it is perfectly reasonable to expect the child to help as well. It is helpful to put a change of dry sheets and nightclothes next to the bed when an alarm is being used; basic forethought can make coping with an alarm at night much easier!

4. Dry and replace the detector. The mat(s) of a bed-type alarm should be wiped dry (this can be done with a dry part of the sheet that has just been wet) and set back up in the bed as before; the detector of a personally worn alarm needs to be wiped dry and fixed back in place with dry pants.

5. Switch the alarm back on, with the on/off switch or by pressing the reset button, depending on the requirements of the particular alarm being used.

6. Return to bed.

Parents (or other helpers) need to do the following while their child is using the alarm:

1. Make sure the alarm is in use and properly set up each night.

2. Avoid 'lifting' the child at night. Don't wake the child to visit the toilet when the alarm has not gone off.

3. Avoid any restrictions on drinking. A child on an alarm should be allowed a drink whenever he or she is thirsty, even last thing at night.

4. Help the child to wake – and go to help quickly. When the parent hears the alarm go off at night, he or she should go as quickly as possible to help the child to wake up, unless the child has already woken and got up. The object is to get the child awake before the bladder

has completely emptied. Where, as will often happen, the alarm has not woken the child by the time a parent gets there, *immediately* waken the child *while the alarm continues to sound*, encouraging him or her to switch it off himself. Guide his or her hand as necessary and assist with the process, but only switch off for the child if he or she is really too unaware of events to do so. Parents should *not* switch off the alarm before waking the child, as this prevents the build-up of the important association between the alarm sound and waking.

5. Remind or guide the child to go to the toilet to finish off.

6. Help the child change bedding and clothing, and replace the alarm box and detector, resetting the alarm. Some children wet more than once in the night, and the alarm should normally be put back in place to 'catch' the next wetting. If, having done this for the first few nights, it is found that the child only wets once in the night, then the child can go back to bed after triggering it without the alarm. This makes for less work at night. Even though catching a second wetting will help the learning of bladder control to progress, a child who usually wets more than once in the night can go back to bed without the alarm after triggering it if bedding or clothing is in short supply, or if the disruption to the sleep of child or parent is proving too much. Children who wet more than once will usually carry on progressing even if only the first wetting each night is 'caught' by the alarm. It is far better to 'miss' the second wetting each night and be able to see treatment through, than to insist on catching the second wetting and give up treatment altogether because the alarm is too disruptive.

7. Help the child to fill in the record chart each morning. Put 'W' for a wet night and 'D' for a dry night (or, if the child is very young, stick on a star or some other stick-on symbol, or colour in the square, for a dry night). Even a small wet patch should be entered as 'W'; for a 'D', the bed must have stayed completely dry all night.

If the alarm gave a 'false alarm', probably triggered by perspiration, there will have been no wet patch with clear edges to it. False alarms should not be recorded as 'Ws' on the chart.

With both bed type and personally worn alarms, the detector mat(s) or plate will need cleaning from time to time. Wipe with warm water, with some washing-up liquid in it if the manufacturer's instructions allow. Disinfectants should not be used on the detector, as they can damage the electrode surface.

A new detector (either a new mat or set of mats, or a new personally worn detector plate, according to the type of alarm in use) should be used for each child treated, for hygiene reasons. The detector is also likely to have taken heavy wear and tear by the end of a full course of treatment. The same alarm box can however be used again with many children.

Older girls are often worried about using an alarm while they have a period. A tampon, however, will not affect urine detection by either the mat(s) of a bed-type of alarm or the detector plate of a personally worn alarm in any way. Urine will 'flood over' other normal types of pad to trigger the alarm, although, of course, the pad will delay things a bit. If by chance blood does reach the detector, all that will happen is a false triggering of the alarm sound.

A parent should always provide the help and supervision described above from the start of treatment. Older children, young people and adults using the alarm may find that they can cope with all the treatment procedures alone, and may prefer to do without a parent or another person being involved at night. However, the alarm user can only cope without help at night if his or her body reacts reliably to the alarm sound by both 'tightening up' and waking up. If it is clear that both these responses do occur regularly, then the alarm user can be offered the option of coping without help at night. It also then becomes possible to use a vibrator-type alarm. Some will be lucky enough to 'tighten up' and wake reliably from the start of treatment. This is a bonus – most will need help in waking (although they may still 'tighten up'), at least at the start of treatment. Those helped as described above (by being woken quickly and while the alarm is still sounding) will in many cases learn to link waking with the alarm sound enough to wake reliably and so be able to cope with the alarm alone at night at a later stage in treatment. Some, regardless of age, always need someone to help them to wake throughout treatment. This does not mean that they are any less likely to become dry, but it does mean that they will not be able to do without a parent's assistance at night. If a child or young person is not confident in coping with the alarm alone, even if they do wake regularly to it, or wake too confused to cope without some assistance, it is important that a parent does continue to give whatever help is needed to ensure that the night-time procedures described above can be followed.

I have met and cured very many children who have had previous bad experiences of trying to use an enuresis alarm. What has often happened is that, without either detailed written guidance or the advice of someone with successful experience of alarm use, the family has fallen into some of the many traps awaiting the unwary alarm user, any one of which can reduce or even destroy the effectiveness of the treatment. In the absence of information or advice to the contrary, the child has often been put to bed with the alarm, with nylon sheets (because they're easy to wash and dry), using a bed-type alarm but wearing pyjama trousers, under the continental quilt he or she always has on the bed. When the alarm has gone off, the parents have waited and waited to see if it is going to 'work' and wake the child, and when it clearly isn't waking him or her, they have eventually gone up to the child, switched the alarm off, and *then* woken the child to change him and the bed. They will not know whether the child is or is not responding to the alarm by 'tightening up', not having been told that this is just as important a reaction to the alarm as waking. After a series of disturbed nights when the alarm went off time and again when the child was dry (after each occasion they have discovered the bed to be dry and so put the child back to sleep in it again regardless of the perspiration in the sheets), they have decided that alarms are not such a good idea after all, and given up, stating that 'the thing never woke him up, so it was useless carrying on'. The tale of woe is all too typical, and it will be similar to the experience of many reading this chapter.

From the guidance already given, it can be seen that, with the best will in the world, using an alarm in this way is destined for disaster and disappointment. The nylon sheets, nylon pyjamas and continental quilt can be relied upon to produce plenty of false alarms through perspiration, while not changing the sheets or reducing the bedding after the first false alarm guarantees that they will carry on happening. The pyjama trousers ensure that the alarm sound will be delayed after wetting has started, while urine has to soak through the extra layer (and an extra layer made of nylon at that, to slow things down still further!), thus making treatment less effective. Waiting to see whether the alarm on its own is going to wake the child, rather than going to help wake the child straight away, weakens the link between the bladder beginning to contract and the child waking, so reducing the learning effect even more, and turning the alarm off before waking the child makes sure that he will not learn to wake up to the alarm. This kind of failure can very easily be replaced by a successful course of alarm treatment, by following the guidance already given.

Signs of progress

Alarm treatment is a process of learning, and each alarm triggering may be seen as another lesson in bladder control for the body. Learning any sort of skill is a gradual process, and the alarm is not a 'magic box' that can produce sudden learning or results. There is no instant cure to bedwetting. Some children do respond more quickly than others, but the average length of treatment is three months, and often no

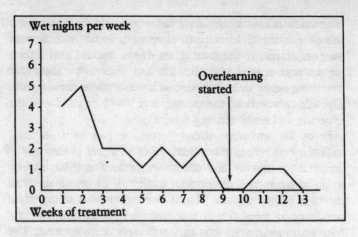

Fig.15 Typical treatment record graph (actual patient)

change is noticed for the first month. The progress made through this learning, as with other forms of learning, is uneven and often includes setbacks as it progresses.

Figure 15 shows a typical graph of wet nights per week during alarm treatment. ('Overlearning' is the procedure designed to increase the chances of staying dry for good, and described in the next section of this chapter, see p. 101.) The graph shown is the actual record of a child treated by the writer, who remained completely dry after treatment.

The following are the most important signs of progress in alarm treatment, although they do not occur in all cases, and do not occur in any given order:

More urine to 'finish off in the toilet'
As the child's wetting is 'turned off' more efficiently and quickly by the tightening up reaction when the alarm goes off, more urine remains in his or her bladder to be emptied on reaching the toilet or pot. If there is any more to be emptied at all, it shows that the child has reacted to the alarm by 'tightening up', even if he or she has not woken

98

without help. Noticing that there is 'more to do' in the toilet after the alarm has gone off is usually one of the first signs that the alarm is having an effect. If the amount left to do in the toilet increases over a few weeks of treatment, the child's body is clearly reacting more quickly to stop the flow of urine – a sign that learning is taking place.

Smaller wet patches

Again, as the child's body learns to shut off the stream of urine more quickly and efficiently, less is emptied into the bed and the wet patch becomes smaller. Usually, the first step is the patch varying in size. It then settles to a more steady reduction in size, so that eventually a child using a bed-type alarm often has wet patches of only saucer (or even coin) size, and a child using a personally worn alarm may only wet the pants and not the bed itself.

Only one wetting per night

Those children who wet more than once each night usually reduce to once only after two to three weeks, if it is possible to use the alarm to 'catch' every wetting.

Better waking to the alarm

Children do not often wake to the alarm without help at first. Some never wake without help, but are cured by the alarm all the same if help arrives fairly quickly. Improved waking often develops during treatment; this is shown by the child often beating his or her parent to the alarm when it is triggered, and being more aware of what is going on once he or she has woken.

Reduced daytime problems

As bladder control begins to improve with the use of an alarm at night, urgency and frequency of visits to the toilet in the daytime, if high to start with, will tend to reduce. This usually happens before much of an increase in dry nights is noticed. Any daytime wetting is likely to improve, and sometimes daytime wetting is cured altogether by night-time alarm treatment.

Wetting later in the night

Wetting (and so the alarm triggering) happening later on in the night than at the start of treatment is a sign of progress, as the child's body copes for longer before losing control and wetting. If wetting and alarm sounds happened before the parents' bedtime at the start of treatment, but after a while start to happen after they have gone to bed, this may be more disruptive of sleep, but it is a good sign that treatment is having an effect!

Self-waking to visit the toilet

The alarm teaches the child's body to hold on to urine and/or to wake up to visit the toilet. Some children hold on more as their main response to treatment, others wake more. Both responses are an acceptable way for the body to keep dry. Waking up more often at night to use the toilet, without wetting and therefore without the alarm going off, is a sign of progress for many children, but it is not one which happens in all cases. Children whose main response to alarm treatment is to learn to hold on rather than wake up may not show this particular sign of progress at all.

More dry nights

This usually follows other signs of progress, and happens most in the second and third months of an average course of treatment. It is of course the sign of progress that everyone looks for, and is the whole point of alarm treatment – but it is important to stress that it is not the only sign of progress. Knowing what else to look for allows both parents and children to spot the evidence that bladder control is being learned from the alarm long before this shows in dry nights on the record chart.

The end of treatment and overlearning

Alarm treatment as described should be continued until the child has been dry for 14 nights *in a row*. This usually takes some eight to twelve weeks, although it can happen quickly for some children who might already have been 'almost there'. It does *not* however take any longer for children whose wetting was more frequent to begin with.

If one stopped using the alarm at the 14 dry nights stage, the chances of renewed wetting in the near future would be around one in three. To reduce this to only a little over one in ten, 'overlearning' should be used, provided there is no medical reason against its use.

Overlearning is an increase in drinking last thing at night before bedtime, while continuing the use of the alarm. This should be started as soon as 14 dry nights have been achieved. While continuing to use the alarm exactly as before, the child should now drink as much as he or she can comfortably manage in the last hour before going to bed. The extra drinks can be spread out over the hour, and he or she can have a variety of different types of drink. It is not necessary to avoid any particular type of drink. Most children and young people manage a pint to a pint and a half – but no more than two pints should be taken in the hour, and the child should *not* drink so much that he or she feels any discomfort. Overlearning aims to get the child to drink more than usual; the object is *not* to drink as much as possible. The extra drinking and continued use of the alarm should be repeated every night.

Overlearning usually causes more wettings and therefore more alarm triggerings (as can be seen in the treatment graph in **Figure 15** on p. 98), but this also means extra lessons in control that build up a safety margin of extra learning to make continued dryness more certain. This was the origin of the term 'overlearning'. Some children are lucky enough to have gained such strong learning during the earlier part of treatment that they remain dry in spite of the extra fluids, while others will need the extra alarm triggerings to train their bodies to cope with the extra load. One likely effect of overlearning is to increase the 'functional capacity' of the bladder (see Chapter Two), and thus the amount of urine it will normally hold, so that the bladder's ability to hold on improves.

Nine out of ten children can cope with overlearning and will become dry again on the alarm even while drinking the extra fluids. If however the child returns to over three wet nights per week on overlearning, or if renewed wetting does not begin to reduce again after two weeks of overlearning, the extra drinking should be stopped. No fluid restrictions should be introduced instead; the child can carry on drinking when he or she is thirsty even last thing at night, but should stop taking the extra. Alarm treatment without overlearning is then continued until a further 14 dry nights in a row are achieved, when treatment can be stopped. Time will have been lost for the one in ten who cannot cope with overlearning, but it is worth trying overlearning for a nine out of ten chance of a significantly longer-lasting cure.

A child who cannot cope with overlearning is not especially likely to relapse into wetting again later. Once he or she has again reached the target of 14 dry nights in a row without overlearning, the chance of relapsing is the same one in three chance that he or she would have had anyway. Before overlearning was introduced into treatment, this was the likelihood of relapse for all children who became dry on the alarm.

Assuming all goes well with overlearning, the alarm and extra fluids at bedtime should be continued until 14 dry nights in a row are again reached. Then both the use of the alarm and the extra fluids may be stopped to finish treatment. After treatment, the child may drink when thirsty, without any fluid restrictions.

Summary: an alarm checklist

- Use the alarm every night
- Do not use nylon sheets or nightclothes
- Do not use a continental quilt
- Reduce amount of bedding and/or room temperature

if the child is hot in bed or sets the alarm off with perspiration

- Do not restrict drinking, even last thing before bedtime
- Change sheets and nightclothes if the alarm is triggered by perspiration (wash them before re-use – don't just dry them out)
- Do not wake the child *unless* the alarm has gone off
- Keep a chart of wet and dry nights (child filling in if possible)

With a bed-type alarm:
- Put the alarm box out of reach or difficult to reach from the bed
- The child should sleep naked below the waist
- The layers on top of the mattress are:

With two detector mats		*With one detector mat*
waterproof		waterproof
first mat	or first mat	detector mat
separating	inside a	bottom sheet
sheet	pillowcase	
second mat		
bottom sheet		

- Flatten the detector mat(s) out carefully in the morning, and occasionally wipe over with warm water

With a personally worn alarm
- Boys and girls will need to wear 2 pairs of pants (not nylon) in bed. For boys the 'briefs' type is better than Y-fronts or boxer shorts, to make sure that the detector plate does not rest against the skin.
- The alarm box is worn:

Sound-type	*Vibrating-type*
On the outside of the pyjama jacket, nightdress, vest or T-shirt, held with Velcro on the soft front area of the shoulder	Inside the pyjama jacket, vest or T-shirt, against the collar bone (so vibration can easily be felt), held by Velcro.

Alternative position – on wrist strap	Alternative positions – on wrist or ankle strap

- The detector plate is worn:
  Taped to front of a pair of pants, over the area which will become wet first
  Wear a *second* pair of pants on top to keep the plate in place
- Do *not* let the plate stay touching the skin at night
- Run the wire *between* the pants, *inside* the pyjama jacket, nightdress, vest or T-shirt
- Wipe the detector occasionally with warm water

When the alarm goes off at night
The child must:

- Switch off the alarm
- Visit the toilet to finish off

The parent should:

- Go to the child *quickly* and help wake him/her
- Leave the alarm sounding while waking up the child, helping him/her to turn it off
- Make sure the child visits the toilet

The child and parent (or the young person coping alone) should then:

- Change the bedclothes and nightclothes as necessary
- Dry the detector mat(s) or plate
- Set the alarm up again, if being used to 'catch' a second wetting in the night

Signs of progress
- 'More to do' in the toilet after waking to the alarm
- Smaller wet patches
- Only one wetting per night (if originally more than one)
- Less help needed to wake to the alarm

- Any daytime wetting, urgency or frequency becomes less
- Wetting happens later in the night
- Child wakes to visit the toilet instead of wetting
- More dry nights

Finishing treatment
- Begin extra drinks (overlearning) in last hour before bed after 14 dry nights in a row
- Stop treatment when dry for 14 nights in a row on extra drinks
- Return to normal drinking if wetting is more than 3 nights in any week with extra drinking, and then stop treatment once again dry for 14 nights in a row

SIX

TROUBLE-SHOOTING
IN ALARM TREATMENT

Most courses of treatment run into problems at some stage, and success depends upon their quick solution. This chapter begins by describing the most common problems and basic ways of dealing with them. A later section deals with the use of an enuresis alarm with a handicapped child.

I have tried in this chapter to give the kind of guidance in 'trouble-shooting' alarm treatment that is likely to be needed by both parents and professionals using alarms with children and young people. I am aware that many readers of this book will be parents who are using an alarm obtained privately, without any professional supervision. For them, I have summarised the experience of a large number of parents using alarms in this way, as a guide to what the family 'working solo' with an alarm at home can expect and in order to identify and guide around the pitfalls that are likely to arise in otherwise unsupervised treatment. The needs of the professional doctor, nurse, or psychologist treating a number of children or running a bedwetting clinic are different. For such professionals I have included guidance on monitoring the treatment of large numbers of patients in the next chapter.

As soon as treatment begins to run into difficulties, it is important to monitor what is happening in more detail than is recorded on the basic 'wet and dry' chart shown in **Figure 10** on p. 72. The detailed treatment record chart shown in **Figure 11** on p. 75 should be used to do this. This chart records not only wet and dry nights, but also keeps a running record of how well the two key bodily reactions of 'tightening up' and waking up are being learned from the alarm. It will identify problems such as non-waking, failure of the stream of urine to be 'shut off' by a muscular tightening up when the alarm goes off, and false alarms. It will also monitor the effectiveness of steps taken, as described later in this chapter, to solve such problems.

Not waking to the alarm

The failure of the enuresis alarm to wake the child is the most frequent reason for people giving up the use of the alarm. It is the most likely problem to be met by those parents and children using an alarm at home without outside supervision, and it is a very common reason given by parents and children who stop attending outpatient bedwetting clinics. All this is a great pity – because difficulty in waking to the alarm is quite usual at first, but usually sorts itself out if the treatment guidance given in the last chapter is followed. Parents and some professionals are not aware that there is another bodily reaction to the alarm (the muscular 'tightening up and stopping the urine stream' reaction) which is just as important as waking, and there are simple ways (described below) of helping a child wake to the alarm.

Few children are always woken by the alarm without the help of a parent, brother or sister at the start of treatment. When I am explaining to my own patients and their parents how to use an alarm, I tell them not to expect the child to wake at all without help in the early stages of treatment; if he or she does wake, this is a bonus. Most children will wake much better as time goes on during treatment, provided parents stick to the routine of going quickly to help the child wake, and never turning the alarm off until the child has been woken up and, with help if needs be, can turn it off himself.

To become dry, a child on alarm treatment must have at least one of the two basic reactions to the alarm sound (or vibration) – that is, he or she must either 'tighten up' or wake up. Most children will develop both during treatment, and this is the ideal, but it is quite common for a child with one but never the other, to be successfully cured. Thus the boy or girl who never wakes without help will probably succeed, provided the alarm causes him or her to stop in midstream. This will be happening satisfactorily if the child has more to do on reaching the toilet after an alarm triggering, and if the wet patch sizes in the bed are becoming smaller. These signs can be monitored by noting them on the detailed record chart (see **Figure 11** on p. 75). If these signs are present, but the child does not wake on his or her own to the alarm, it is enough to continue simply waking the child as soon as the alarm goes off, helping him to wake, then helping him in turning off the alarm, and always going quickly to the child when you hear the alarm rather than waiting to see if he or she will wake on his own. Any progress in the child's body waking to the alarm without someone else's help will be seen from the detailed chart, which allows a record to be kept of how often the child beats his or her parent to the off-switch.

Some children are still very confused and sleepy even when woken by a parent after the alarm has gone off. They need physical guidance to switch off the alarm and visit the toilet, and, with a personally worn alarm, to cope with the detector plate and pants. Without someone to help, some children will be sufficiently confused to begin getting ready for school, or to try using a non-existent toilet unless guided to the real one. Guidance is needed, but the alarm will not harm a child who is always in a sleepy and confused state when he or she is woken by it, or is helped to wake by a parent.

Where a child is confused on waking at night, it is useful to give the child some intensive practice at getting from the bed to the toilet and back, so that this will become more automatic – and more likely to happen even when the child is only partially wakened by a full bladder. The training is essentially the 'positive practice' part of the 'dry bed training' treatment described in Chapter Three. Children will understand that in order to learn an action in a sport, or a piece of music, you will practice over and again until the action or piece of music becomes automatic. Many children will have learned complicated bits of music, actions in football, moves in gymnastics, strokes in swimming, or the like in this way. Getting to the toilet can be practiced until it is automatic, in the same way. Every night for a week, the child should be asked to practice getting out of bed, going to the toilet, standing or sitting there as if to urinate, and getting back to bed afterwards, ten times over, before finally settling down to sleep (not, of course, forgetting to set the alarm up after the 'ten times practice' session!). Each of the ten times practice trips to the toilet should be carried out at the speed the child would really walk to the toilet – avoiding the temptation to run like a relay race to get the practice over quickly!

Most of us have experienced finding ourselves turning the wrong way or running into a wall when we are visiting the toilet at night in a strange building, because we automatically follow what would be our usual route to the toilet at home. This is the automatic route that this practice routine aims to strengthen for the child who does not automatically get to the toilet when he or she is partially awakened by an active bladder, but is confused or wandering at night.

Some children, in a sleepy state, naturally switch off an alarm box next to the bed, but do not then complete the procedure by visiting the toilet to finish off. They are then quite likely to wet again later in the night, but this time in an already wet bed and without the benefit of the alarm. Putting the alarm behind a piece of furniture against the wall, so that it can only be switched off after getting out of bed is a crude but effective way of ensuring that the child does complete the process (see **Figure 16** on p. 121).

If difficulty in waking remains a problem, particularly if the child is not regularly responding to the alarm by shutting off the stream of urine, then any of the following may be used to assist the child's body to wake to the alarm. Choose which to start with according to what is most feasible under the circumstances, and monitor its effects on both waking and the 'tightening up' response on the detailed chart. Many of these changes aim to improve the child's response to the alarm by changing the sound of the alarm. It is important to remember that, apart from extremely loud alarms, it is the *right* sound, rather than the *loudest* sound, that is being sought:

1. Adjust the alarm sound, if the alarm box has this facility.
2. Change alarms – even two alarms of the same type will give very different sounds.
3. If using a bed-type alarm, stand the alarm box on a different type of surface – such as a metal tray – which will make a surprising difference to the noise it makes.
4. Put the alarm box of a bed-type alarm inside an open biscuit tin, to change the sound even more.
5. If using a personally worn alarm, change the position of the alarm box.
6. Change the battery in the alarm box. It is easy to overlook a run-down battery, but this will reduce the sound or vibration of any alarm.
7. On a bed-type alarm with the necessary facility, use a plug-in booster buzzer or vibrator box (attached to the bedhead or under the pillow). The accessory used *must* be the right one for the equipment being used.
8. Check that the procedures are being followed correctly, and that you are not falling into one of the pitfalls that make waking more difficult – like using nylon sheets or nightclothes, or a child using a bed-type of alarm wearing pyjama trousers, pants or a long nightdress in bed.
9. Switch from one type of alarm to another, from a bed-type alarm to a personally worn alarm, or vice versa.
10. If using the sound type of alarm, switch to using a personally worn vibrating alarm.
11. Train the child's body to link waking with the alarm going off, by triggering the alarm each morning ·and waking the child for the day while the alarm is still going. (This is more suitable with a bed-type of alarm, where there is a test button to trigger the alarm. For

a personally worn alarm, a second alarm unit will be needed for the parent to trigger in the morning.)

If none of the above methods produces any improvement in waking, but the child is still stopping the urine stream when the alarm goes off, there is little cause for concern. If, however, there are no other signs of progress, and particularly if there is no more to do on reaching the toilet, or parents do not hear the alarm to go to help the child, some children can be taught to wake to an alarm sound by being woken at two or three randomly-spaced times each night (between their bedtime and that of their parents). Again, this is easier to do if you are using a bed-type of alarm, where there is a test button to press on the alarm box which triggers the sound. The parent should start the alarm, then wake the child up while it is sounding. The child may then switch off the alarm (with help if needed), and visit the toilet if he or she wants to. The alarm should be reset to catch any wetting later in the night as usual. This routine may be tried for two or three weeks, and its effects on waking to a 'real' alarm triggering on a wet night monitored on the detailed chart.

If none of the above methods produces any improvement in waking, *and* there is still no progress, do not despair. Continue using the alarm for the average treatment period of three months, keeping the detailed record chart to detect the beginnings of any of the necessary responses. If there is still no progress after this period take a break from the alarm for three months, then try again. Previous failures to respond to an alarm do not mean that a further attempt at the same treatment will automatically fail.

Not shutting off the stream of urine

The reaction of shutting off the stream of urine, by tightening up the muscles of the pelvic floor between the legs beneath the bladder (and around the urethra leading from the bladder), is the other central 'building block' of alarm treatment. Its occurrence can be monitored by recording on the detailed chart the size of the wet patch and the amount of urine still left to do in the toilet after the child has been woken to the alarm. If progress is slow and the detailed chart shows that this reaction is not, or is very rarely occurring, the steps just described to help with non-waking should be tried to help the stimulus of the alarm to get through.

If these do not have an effect on the recorded signs of tightening up and shutting off, the following special training routine can be used, and its effects monitored on the detailed chart, over a period of two to three weeks. The purpose is to train the child's body to link tightening up with the sound (or vibration) of the alarm, and to increase the chances of the child's body recalling the link when the alarm goes off for real at night. This routine should not be used if there is any indication that the child's daytime bladder emptying is in any way abnormal (eg. the stream of urine is usually unsteady or interrupted). Check with the doctor before using this technique to avoid any doubt about this.

On at least one visit the child makes to the toilet to empty his or her bladder each day while at home (most conveniently in the evening), he or she should be accompanied by a parent (or brother or sister) carrying the alarm box. The alarm should be set off by the parent as soon as the child has started the urine stream into the toilet. On bed-type alarms, this can be done simply by pressing the test button (without the mats being connected to the box, or if they are left on, making sure that they are not touching, as that will either trigger the alarm too soon, or stop the test button from triggering it, depending on the make of alarm). With a personally worn alarm, the alarm can be triggered by touching the detector plate with wet fingers. With a sound-type alarm, the parent can trigger the alarm sound just outside the open toilet or bathroom door. With a vibrating type of personal alarm, the child will need to hold the alarm box in its usual position against the collar-bone, or to wear it on the wrist or ankle strap.

As soon as the parent has triggered the alarm, the child

should try to 'shut off' the flow of urine by tightening up the muscles between the legs. (Boys need to be told not to cheat by squeezing the penis instead.) If he or she succeeds, the alarm should be turned off and urination then be completed – with congratulations on a task well-achieved!

General lack of progress

Sometimes a child's basic responses of stopping the stream and waking to the alarm seem to be happening strongly enough, but treatment nevertheless does not seem to be getting anywhere. Perhaps the child has made some progress at first, but then seems to have got 'stuck' on a plateau, and progress has stopped.

In this situation, it is well worth changing the type of alarm being used, to give the child a different and possibly more effective (for him or her) 'jumping and waking' stimulus that might get through better, always monitoring the effects of any change made on a detailed record chart. It is also possible to increase the chances of an alarm stimulus having a stonger impact on jumping and waking by using *two* alarms at the same time. The child can wear a personally worn alarm while also sleeping on a bed alarm, or can even wear both a sound-type and a vibrating-type of personally worn alarm. In the first combination, the child will be given two very different types of sound, and the bed alarm will go off a few seconds after the personally worn alarm (because it takes the urine longer to soak through – particularly as the child will now be wearing two pairs of pants). In effect, two chances at both jumping to stop the stream and waking, instead of the usual one. With a combination of two types of personally worn alarm, the child gets the benefit of two very different inputs from the alarms at almost the same time – again, doubling the chances of getting through.

Another strategy where the child is just not progressing on a standard alarm is to give him or her a 'booster' course of training, with a modified version of the 'dry bed training' treatment described in Chapter Three, as an addition to using the alarm in the normal way. A useful booster adaptation of the waking component of this is to wake the child three times, at hourly intervals after he or she has settled to sleep but before the parents' own bedtime, for a week (if necessary, and if this helps, a second one week course can be added after a week's 'recovery break'). If possible, trigger the alarm and then wake the child to the sound, to help strengthen the waking response at the same time. This can be done with the test button of a bed alarm, or by using a second alarm unit of the same type as the child is wearing if a personally worn alarm is being used.

When the child is as awake as possible, take him or her *halfway* to the toilet, and ask him to do a 'bladder check' – to tell you whether he or she feels the need to go to the toilet or not. You can practice the idea of a 'bladder check' like this in the day, to help get the idea. Many children will not be very communicative (to say the least!) at this point, so the parent can accept a non-verbal 'voting with the feet', like simply wandering back to bed or in the general direction of the toilet; but be prepared to guide the child en route if necessary.

The reason for taking the child halfway to the toilet before doing the bladder check is that this makes it more of a real decision – ask a child at the toilet, and he or she will tend to 'go' anyway, and ask a child still in bed and they will tend to simply turn over and go back to sleep regardless! The child should be congratulated whichever decision he or she makes. Do not be tempted to say 'now you're up, you may as well go', even if the child often wets later the same night: the idea is not to get urine into the toilet instead of the bed each night, but to give the child night-time practice at checking whether his or her bladder is squeezing ready to empty, remembering that research studies have indicated that the waking routine was the most effective element in the 'dry bed training' treatment.

Where there is not time to fit in three wakings between the child's bedtime and the parents', or where this waking routine is making the child too tired, two rather than three wakings can be tried for a week. Even one waking is worth trying, although with only one waking the time should be varied from night to night to avoid things degenerating into a single regular time for emptying the bladder, which could be counterproductive.

Finally for the child who is simply not progressing on alarm treatment, it is worth checking the obvious and reviewing exactly how the alarm is being used, and whether the child is still wearing the right nightclothes for the alarm. It is amazing how often what is actually happening has 'drifted' from what is supposed to be happening! Both parents and professionals should find the Progress Form given in the next chapter useful in carrying out this kind of stock-take of treatment.

Damaged or worn detector mats

On bed-type alarms, one detector mat (or set of detector mats) is not always enough to last a complete course of treatment, although the durability of different types of mat varies. Mats tend to last longer if the bed they are on is firm and flat, rather than sagging in the middle, and if they are not too often jumped on by the child using the bed for gymnastics practice!

Damaged or worn bed mats should be replaced. Single mat types can become unreliable if the electrode strips are broken. Broken wires on mesh types can disrupt treatment by producing false alarms when the child gets into bed, or by putting the alarm temporarily out of action by a short-circuit between the two mats, and the broken ends are uncomfortable and scratchy. As a temporary measure while getting new mats, a small broken area on a wire mesh mat can be covered with a piece of waterproof sticking-plaster.

False alarms

Alarms do sometimes trigger on a bed that has not been wet, and in some courses of treatment such false alarms can become a major problem. False alarms should not be counted as wettings on the record chart. It is very common for children not to be woken by a false alarm, even if they normally wake well to the alarm, because the alarm sound or vibration is not linked in a false alarm to the sensation of a full bladder. A child woken by a false alarm does not need to visit the toilet if he or she does not want to.

As has been noted in the previous chapter, the usual cause of false alarms is dampening of the detector by perspiration, and a number of standard precautions need to be taken to avoid this becoming a problem. Any body fluid, apart from the usual ones of urine and perspiration, can trigger an alarm, however, and blood or saliva (perhaps on a well-sucked thumb!) can cause false alarms. Faulty or over-sensitive alarm equipment is a less common but possible cause. The following are the steps to take if false alarms are proving a problem:

1. On bed-type alarms with twin mats, check for short-circuits because of broken wires poking through the separating sheet between wire-mesh mats, or because of a threadbare or holed separating sheet allowing the mats to touch. Clip off any broken wires and cover the area with a sticking-plaster until replaced with new mats. Replace a threadbare or holed separating sheet with a better one. If the child's movement at night is causing the mats to touch each other, put the lower mat inside a pillowcase.

2. Reduce perspiration by reducing the quantity of bedding and the bedroom temperature, if excessive. Avoid waterproof-encased mattresses, which can be hotter to sleep on than a normal mattress covered with a single waterproof sheet. The need to avoid continental quilts has already been mentioned.

3. Follow strictly the guidance already given that the bottom sheet, any separating sheet, and any pants being worn with a personal alarm, should be removed after a false alarm and *washed*, rather than just dried out, before re-use. Putting the child straight back into bed with the same sheet or pants that have just caused a false alarm, or re-using the same sheets or pants after drying

the perspiration out on a radiator, is very tempting, but this will lead to repeated false alarms. Sheets or pants damp enough with perspiration to cause one false alarm do not need much more perspiration to cause another, and the salty deposits remain in the material even after it is dried out.

4. With a personally worn alarm, it is possible for the few drops of urine left 'in the tubes' after a perfectly normal visit to the toilet to cause enough dampness to trigger the alarm after going back to bed. This is not a common problem, but can easily be resolved by changing the position of the detector plate slightly so that it is a little further from the outlet of the urethra.

5. Reduce alarm sensitivity and absorb more of the perspiration by putting more absorbent material between the child and the detector. On bed-type alarms, this is done by doubling (or even tripling) the thickness of separating sheet between the mats of twin mat alarms, or of the bottom sheet over the mat of single mat alarms, or by allowing the child to wear pyjama trousers (in preference to pants, as pyjama trousers cover more of the child and therefore protect against more of the perspiration). The pyjama trousers used should not be made of nylon.

With personally worn alarms, moving the detector plate to a slightly higher position on the front of the pants often helps. While more than one extra layer of material can easily be put between the child and the detector on bed-type alarms, it is not practicable to ask the child to wear more than two pairs of pants because not only would it be more uncomfortable, but it would also be counterproductive in making the child more likely to perspire.

6. If false alarms persist and none of the above ploys reduces the problem to an acceptable level, it is possible that the alarm is unusually sensitive, and it would be useful to try a different alarm, either of the same type, or of a different type altogether. Some manufacturers are able

to adjust the sensitivity of their alarms, and *in extremis* it is worth asking whether this can be done.

Alarm failure

If the alarm does not go off when the child has wet, and you have checked that it has been set up properly, it may be tested quickly by one of the following methods:

on bed-type alarms, by pressing the test button on the alarm box (according to the manufacturer's instructions). Keep the detector mat terminals apart when doing this. On many alarms, the equipment can be tested by touching the terminals together; but check the manufacturer's instructions as this will not work with all alarms.

on bed alarms, by setting the alarm up in the bed and pouring enough *salty* water onto the bottom sheet to make a wet patch, then pressing on the patch with firm hand pressure for a few seconds.

with personal alarms, by firmly holding the detector plate with wet fingers (saliva will do, but water is more hygienic!).

The following causes should be checked and put right if possible if the alarm still fails to work:

1. Mats on a twin mat alarm not properly placed one above the other.
2. Mats on a twin mat alarm being accidentally connected (short-circuited) together by a broken piece of wire mesh or touching through a threadbare or holed separating sheet.
3. A poor or broken connection between the connecting cable and either the alarm box or the detector.
4. Run-down battery.
5. Damage to the alarm box if it has been dropped or roughly handled.
6. The detector plate wire not being firmly plugged into the alarm box, on certain types of personal alarms.
7. The Stop/Reset button on a personal alarm being jammed

against the casing – it is usually easy to free.

Note that it is not unknown for someone (patient, brother or sister perhaps) to turn off the alarm before settling to sleep at night!

Relapse after treatment

After completing treatment, the occasional wet night as things settle down is quite common and nothing to worry about.

Most children who have not had a bedwetting 'problem' have the very occasional wet night, and seven out of ten children will have an *occasional* wet night after successful treatment without this developing any further into a return of regular bedwetting. For the child who does restart regular wetting in the future (this happens with about 13 per cent of the children successfully treated with overlearning), this is disappointing but not a disaster. He or she will probably respond to a second course of treatment as well as to the first, and is no more likely to relapse after that than any other child being treated for the first time. There are not many children I have ever had to treat more than twice before they became reliably dry.

A second course of treatment should be considered if wetting has returned for one or more nights per week on average. This can be checked by restarting a simple 'wet and dry' chart, which as has been noted can help to reduce problems again even by itself.

At the end of a successful course of treatment with overlearning, all children have a nearly nine out of ten chance of remaining dry without needing any further treatment or special effort. Relapses can happen simply because bladder control has always been a difficult skill for children who have been bedwetters, or can be triggered by something stressful or a straightforward and non-stressful change of circumstances. Relapses mean nothing more than that some children must be expected to need two sessions rather than one of training in bladder control before the skill is secure. That is not the child's fault, and which children will need a second course of treatment cannot be predicted beforehand. Refresher courses are a part of learning and holding onto many kinds of skill.

Alarm treatment with the handicapped child

Alarm treatment can be used quite successfully with children having a variety of mental or physical handicaps. In the case of a physically handicapped child (or adult), the doctor should be consulted over the suitability of the alarm. Broadly however, treatment can usually be adapted around a handicap that affects mobility (by counting on parental help to switch off the alarm and by use of a bottle or other receptacle for urination where the toilet cannot be reached). In the case of a handicap in which the physical aspects of bladder control are affected (as in some forms of paralysis), control may be impossible and the alarm therefore inappropriate. There are some marginal cases however in which a doctor may consider that an alarm may help to make the best use of what ability to control has been left by a partial impairment. As has already been said, deafness is no longer an obstacle to alarm treatment with the introduction of personal vibrator alarms, and if the child needs help in waking, a bed-type alarm with the facility for a plug-in vibrator unit gives the best of both worlds. The vibrator unit is likely to produce a response from the child, while the accompanying standard alarm sound summons assistance.

The sound-type of alarm is a suitable treatment for mentally handicapped children, provided its use is practicable with the particular child. Although the treatment relies on learning, it is such basic body-learning that success does not require high levels of intelligence, and can be achieved despite a mental handicap.

Special allowances do have to be made in treating a mentally handicapped child, however. Explanation is likely to be difficult, and a seriously handicapped child may not be able to take an active role in his or her treatment. The alarm's presence and its sound often need introducing *gradually*, in

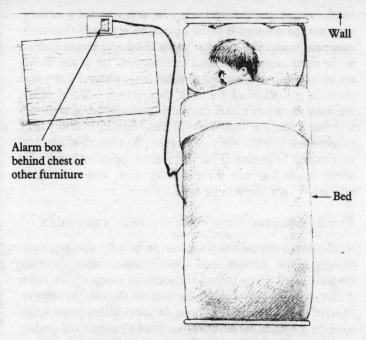

Wall

Alarm box
behind chest or
other furniture

Bed

**Fig.16   Alarm box behind furniture to make sure the
child leaves the bed to switch off**

small doses rather than suddenly. The alarm can be placed
and sounded at a considerable distance from the child at first,
while he or she is happy at something else, and brought closer
in stages when he or she accepts it without fear. It can then
be set up in the bedroom. Parents will need to help most
mentally handicapped children to wake, switching the alarm
off after waking and guiding to the toilet or pot. Sometimes
a child will chew the alarm lead, and this can often be routed
under the bed and taped to avoid tempting lengths of lead. If
the alarm box itself is a source of temptation, or is 'hauled in'
for attention on the end of its lead, it can often be wedged on
the floor behind a piece of furniture angled to the wall as in
Figure 16.

In treating a mentally handicapped child, one must look

out for inappropriate reactions to the alarm, and if necessary, abandon the attempt if these cannot be resolved. One fairly common problem of this sort is the child who remains afraid of the alarm despite a gradual introduction. He or she should not be pushed, or future and possibly more successful attempts might be prejudiced. A second is the child who actually enjoys the noise the alarm makes too much, and will deliberately urinate when awake to hear it go off! This learning is hardly to be encouraged. If such difficulties occur, the chances of eventual success will be greater if the treatment is postponed and tried afresh in not less than three months' time, when the child's reaction is very likely to be quite different.

Parents using the alarm without outside supervision

While many alarms are issued to parents by doctors, community health services, and special clinics, many more are bought, hired or borrowed privately by parents who either prefer to treat their children themselves without the involvement of outsiders, or who obtain an alarm if they come across too long a waiting list to obtain one from a professional source.

As has already been said, it is important that parents wishing to obtain an alarm privately and to treat their child without outside supervision (or an adult wishing to treat him- or herself alone) should first check with the doctor that the treatment is suitable for the child concerned, that the child does not have an infection of the urinary tract (or if he or she does, that the doctor will treat it as appropriate), and that the equipment to be used meets the latest safety requirements. Do not buy or hire anything other than currently produced equipment from a reputable manufacturer which is clearly stated to conform to current DoH safety specifications; older equipment that someone else may offer to give or lend may not be safe, and could cause skin damage.

Parents who use enuresis alarms they have obtained privately for their children can obtain results that are almost as good as those obtained by the best professional clinics. A properly run enuresis clinic would expect around 80 per cent of its child patients to become dry with alarm treatment. In my own recent research into how parents fared with privately obtained alarms, I found that of those that persevered, just over 70 per cent succeeded in getting their children dry. Between one in three and one in four did give up the alarm treatment – mostly because of the alarm's failure to wake the child. One should note, however, that even in professionally run clinics, one often comes across a similarly high rate of families giving up treatment.

From this research, parents using alarms privately can expect a one in four chance that they will need to meet the problem of the alarm failing to wake the child. This is likely to be their major difficulty. The advice given on alarm use in the last chapter, and the advice on trouble-shooting given in this chapter, are intended to help overcome this problem. It is clear from the reports sent in by parents about their experiences in using the alarm in this research study, that the natural reaction to hearing an enuresis alarm going off may not help the child to wake to it. Four out of ten parents waited to see if the alarm would wake the child on its own rather than going quickly to help the child, and one in six regularly turned off the alarm before waking the child. That it is important to follow the guidance given on these points was underlined by the fact that the parents of children who failed to become dry on the alarm in this study were twice as likely to have 'waited to see' whether the alarm would wake them rather than going quickly to help, and four times as likely to have switched the alarm off *before* waking the child, compared with the children who became dry on the alarm.

From this survey, parents using alarms privately to treat their children's bedwetting are likely to have someone giving them advice on a personal basis on how to use the alarm. Approximately half do have someone able to offer professional advice, and about one in six use the advice of other parents who have experience of using the alarm. About half, however, start treatment without getting a sample of the child's urine checked for possible infection, and four out of ten do not keep any form of record of how the child is progressing in treatment. I hope that the advice given in this book will enable parents wishing to treat their own children privately to achieve greater success. It cannot of course foresee or advise on how to avoid some of the more unusual pitfalls that may arise – like the problem reported by one parent when on the first night of treatment, the child's grandfather rushed into the street when the alarm went off, believing the house to be on fire!

SEVEN

RUNNING AN ENURESIS CLINIC

It is beyond the scope of this book to give anything other than a few key points on running a professional enuresis clinic. These may be of assistance to the doctor, community nurse or psychologist who has successfully treated a series of children with the alarm and is considering setting up a special clinic.

Equipping the clinic

In equipping a clinic, it is valuable to purchase a range of enuresis alarm equipment, sufficient to be in a position to offer the choice between personally worn and bed-type alarms in all cases, and to have the facility to swop between one type and the other if necessary during treatment. The clinic should have enough plug-in vibrator boxes and booster buzzers for bed-type alarms and vibrator personal alarms to enable these options to be used with children or young people with a particular need for this type of equipment from the outset, or who have a poor response to the standard sound type of equipment.

All equipment purchased should conform to the current DoH specifications regarding safety, to reduce the likelihood of skin ulceration or burns through electrical current passing between electrodes in contact with the skin. At the time of writing, the current government guidance is embodied in performance specification R/E 1004/03, issue II of 1988 (see Appendix p. 169). Some professionals are faced with an 'inheritance' of older enuresis alarm equipment and too small a budget for wholesale replacement. In these circumstances it is *essential* that the equipment be checked against the latest DoH specifications, as many of the types of alarm in use in some clinics a few years ago do not conform to safety requirements, and some have been responsible for serious skin damage. Such equipment should be destroyed.

It is essential in running the clinic to keep a stock of replacement detectors, batteries and alarms, so that any breakdowns can be replaced immediately without introducing a delay in treatment. There is nothing quite so demoralising as having to wait weeks while the clinic gets hold of a replacement alarm after a breakdown (perhaps by waiting for another patient to finish with one). It is also obviously preferable to be able to replace a broken alarm with another of the same type, so that changes in alarm type are planned according to preference, practicalities and treatment requirements, rather than forced upon the patient by a shortage of replacement equipment. Avoid the temptation to carry out repairs, adaptations and adjustments not allowed for in the manufacturer's instructions, because of the danger of affecting the safety provisions of the alarm. It is useful to establish contact with the equipment manufacturer for repairs, replacements and adjustments (the one you might need to request is to the sensitivity of some alarms).

With a large number of alarms issued, some losses are to be expected (I am amazed at how many of my past patients appear to have left the area complete with enuresis alarm!), but it is also all too easy to lose track of equipment, especially if there are arrangements to 'drop it in' once treatment is completed. Numbering alarms and keeping a log of their locations separately from individual treatment records helps, and where it is feasible patients may be asked to bring the alarm with them to each appointment.

Clinic organization

The financial arrangements for a clinic need to cover not only capital funds to buy equipment in the first place, but also revenue for printing record forms, replacement of equipment, and to provide new detector mat(s) or plates for each patient's treatment (plus replacements for detectors failing during treatment). Printed checklists of treatment instructions and a supply of printed 'wet/dry' and more detailed record charts (perhaps on the models of those reproduced in this book) are essential. Space can usefully be left on the bottom of record charts to write a reminder of any major changes to treatment – such as the instructions for overlearning or for practising waking or stopping the stream of urine to the alarm.

Before seeing the first patients, it is essential to make satisfactory arrangements to secure physical examination and medical clearance for the treatment of each child, and for taking and dealing with the laboratory report on midstream urine samples from each child. These arrangements will depend on one's own profession and position.

It is important to give each family a wet/dry chart to fill in *before* considering the start of treatment, so that a baseline record is available of pre-treatment wetting frequency as part of the initial assessment. I find it helpful to secure at least two weeks' records by sending a chart with the letter inviting the patient to a first appointment.

There are many different models for running a bedwetting clinic. Some see all the patients regularly at outpatient appointments, others work entirely through home visiting, and some through a combination of the two. What is appropriate naturally depends on local circumstances – and resources, since the staffing requirements are very different for different models of running a clinic. Whichever clinic model is adopted, however, it is essential to allow sufficient time to assess the child and the situation before deciding whether alarm treatment is appropriate and practical, and to explain to *both* child and parent(s) what the problem of bedwetting is likely to be in his or her case, how treatment is intended to work, exactly how to use the equipment, and what difficulties there may be in the early stages (so that these do not come as a demoralising surprise and there is a means of countering them). I find an hour is the minimum to do this properly. It is also important to keep in contact once the alarm is in use, to monitor progress and deal with any problems and necessary changes to treatment. This may be by clinic appointments or domiciliary visits, but many have found it necessary to arrange contact with each family at least once each fortnight. Things drift if contact, and resolution of any problems in treatment, becomes less frequent than this. Consideration does of course need to be given to how to follow up those who stop attending the clinic if an outpatient appointment model is being followed; treatment may be continuing unsupervised, it may have been defeated by unresolved problems (which may or may not prove resolvable), and there is potentially the loss of an alarm involved.

I have found effective a clinic model which has a central outpatient clinic for initial assessments, explanation and demonstration of treatment procedures, and major reviews of treatment (for overlearning, or when there are significant treatment difficulties), together with fortnightly domiciliary supervision visiting carried out by community nursing staff. It is often helpful for any clinic to provide a guide and monitoring pro forma for use by professional staff undertaking home visits to supervise alarm treatment, particularly for use by professional staff doing such visits as part of a hard-pressed day, and who have not had detailed training in enuresis treatment. At the end of this chapter I have reproduced a Progess Form, based on that used for some years in my own clinical work. This form can be used by professionals on supervisory home visits and by staff checking progress and problems at routine clinic appointments. The form acts as an *aide memoire* on treatment procedures, a checklist to run through with child and parent to identify both signs of treatment progress and any problems needing to be dealt with, and 'first aid' guidance on on-the-spot countermeasures to some of the more common treatment difficulties (both in treatment response and household practicalities). Printed on a self-carboned pad to produce automatic duplicates, the form has served well as both a treatment record form for the visiting supervisor and a report on progress to a central clinic or specialist, where it can indicate whether a problem is remaining unresolved and a specialist review is needed. Different people work in different ways (and have differing degrees of allergy to standard forms!), but I hope that the form will be of assistance as a possible starting-point in designing a monitoring process for some who are establishing a bedwetting clinic.

Assessment

The content of the assessment of enuresis needed to decide whether the alarm is suitable for a particular patient, the need for additional medical assessment if you are not medically qualified, and the treatment guidance to be given will be clear from the preceding chapters. Demonstration of the alarm, rather than just a description or written instructions, is essential – far too many alarms are still issued with little or no demonstration, and parents left to follow little more than the manufacturer's instructions or brief printed notes. Even worse, staff with scant previous experience of alarm use find themselves landed with the task of issuing alarms. It will also be clear that alarms should not be issued for a standard period of time, but rather for the duration of a course of treatment which should continue while there are good signs of progress, or until a proper clinical decision is made on monitoring information that treatment is not going to achieve its goal.

Assessment needs to establish the baseline level of wetting, and for monitoring purposes the presence or absence of daytime wetting or daytime urgency or frequency of urination. The presence or absence of faecal soiling should also be established: a bedwetting clinic is an acceptable place to be asking about other forms of continence; faecal soiling is more common among bedwetting children than the general population; and if it is there it is a sufficiently serious and demoralising problem to merit separate referral and treatment.

Factors to be explored on the nature of the enuresis itself, with indications as to the type of problem the child has (which can be explained to him or her) are its history (to identify primary or secondary enuresis – both of which will respond equally well to treatment), possible regular patterns (particularly differences between term-time and holidays, and any reduction in wetting when away from home), and whether there is a family history of enuresis. Abnormalities in urination, pain on passing urine, diabetes or other possibly related conditions, fits or a history of urinary tract infection need medical assessment.

From the point of view of designing the treatment and selecting the appropriate alarm type, the experience of any previous alarm treatment needs to be considered, as do sleeping arrangements in the house (check for accessibility to a toilet or pot, availability of extra sheets and washing facilities, readiness to use the toilet with or without problems of fear of the dark, acceptability of the alarm sound disturbing sleep of anyone else in the room and to parents, whether the child has his or her own bed, ease of helping the child when the alarm goes off and who will normally do this, type of bedding, whether the child will be concerned at sleeping naked below the waist on a bed-type of alarm, and where the alarm box is going to be put or worn – top bunk beds can be a problem in locating a bed-type alarm!). Note that it is *not* necessary for children on the alarm to have their own room.

Take the child's preferences into account in deciding alarm type, and in agreeing arrangements for visiting the toilet. Some children sleeping a distance from the toilet (particularly if it is on another floor or outside) strongly prefer to go there nevertheless, while others equally strongly prefer to have a pot or bucket in the bedroom. Simple practicalities like this may appear minor, but agreeing on them at the outset can avoid later misunderstandings, failures to carry out the necessary procedures, and even arguments.

To assist in monitoring progress, it is important to ask before treatment begins whether there have been any recent changes in the wetting frequency or pattern (you may be starting treatment on either an upward or downward trend), and how often the child normally wakes unaided to use the toilet at night, responding to bladder stimuli alone. One in five bedwetting children will regularly self-wake in this way.

In order to give the necessary treatment advice, you will need to cover in the initial assessment whether the child is already on any treatment or special routine for bedwetting, and in particular whether he or she is being lifted at night or is having fluids restricted, either generally or last thing at night. Existing treatments obviously need to be consulted about with the responsible person, and information from any previous investigations into bedwetting (particularly if they involved hospital investigations) needs to be obtained.

During treatment, one should expect a proportion of families to give up. This drop-out rate is likely to be in the region of one patient in three and, not surprisingly, is related to lack of progress in treatment and in particular to unresolved failure of the alarm to wake the child. Interestingly, it is also more likely in families where bedwetting is common in other members of the family, and is seen as more of a usual part of growing up than as a special problem; in these circumstances, the family will probably have experience of children 'growing out' of bedwetting, and may well see the treatment as more of a problem than the wetting itself.

Families where parents are intolerant of the problem of bedwetting are more likely to drop out of treatment. The most important factors likely to be linked to a poor response to the alarm are, again, unresolved failure of the alarm to wake the child, and the existence of problems in the family. As has been said already, it is helpful to avoid starting treatment at an unusually stressful time, seeing whether there is any way of helping to overcome stress that the child and family may be under, and if there is not, ensuring that problems in treatment, and particularly in waking the child up, are resolved wherever possible and as quickly as possible so that families with other problems do not also have to cope with any avoidable treatment difficulties.

Clinic policies

A key policy issue for the professional setting up an enuresis clinic is that he or she will need to decide from the outset whether the clinic is going to treat bedwetting *only*, or whether it will also treat daytime wetting and faecal soiling. The necessary expertise and medical input will be needed for these. These problems will very soon be found among bedwetting children attending any clinic, and if they cannot be treated a decision needs to be made about where families with these problems will be referred for help. It is also necessary from the outset to decide whether the clinic will offer *only* alarm treatment, and refer children for whom an alarm is not appropriate or is impractical elsewhere; or whether the medical input to follow other courses of treatment, particularly the prescription of drugs, can be laid on.

All contact with the patient should not be stopped once he or she has become dry on the alarm. Just over one in ten of those patients finishing treatment with a successful period of overlearning will need a second course of treatment, as will approximately one in three of those who did not manage overlearning. A follow-up system needs to be established, both to offer further help to those who need it, and to ensure that the relapse rate is taken into account in any assessment of the clinic's success rate. A simple letter, ideally reply-paid, six months after stopping treatment is appropriate. If this is not possible, then at least the contact number for any further help should be given to all departing patients, and the advice given that very occasional wet nights should not cause undue worry, regular wettings should again be recorded on a chart (which will help), and that the need for a second course of treatment does exist and will be met if it is requested.

A final policy issue is that of consistency of treatment personnel. Treatment of enuresis relies to a significant extent on the family's confidence and application of techniques at home, and is known to be significantly affected by the attitudes of both child patient and parents. It is important that, as far as possible, the family is supported by the same therapist throughout treatment. I find that many patients arriving at my own clinic are critical of the inconsistency of support they have received in previous treatments when they were seen by different professionals at successive visits to a clinic or hospital, often receiving conflicting advice at successive appointments. This can be as problematic as general lack of supervision. It is equally important that all those who treat enuresis at a clinic, or through community domiciliary services, should have been specifically trained in the treatment of enuresis and the specific techniques offered, and that supervision of new and less experienced therapists should be available from more experienced staff with a proven track record in treating bedwetting successfully.

Monitoring

It is important, both for the patients treated and for the efficient and effective use of resources, that the overall effectiveness of the clinic is monitored. It is also important that families should be told what the clinic's success rate and average duration of treatment is. At its simplest, the operation of a clinic can be monitored by aggregating individual patient statistics. Use of common national definitions of factors such as treatment success, drop out, and relapse is strongly to be advocated to enable comparisons between clinics as well as consistent appraisal of the clinic's operations over time – without these, it is all too possible for either a glowing or a gloomy picture to emerge quite unjustifiably by a quirk of the definitions used. It is, for example, possible for a clinic to claim 100 per cent success rate, quite unjustifiably, simply by carrying on with everyone's treatment until they either become dry, or drop out of treatment – and then excluding patients who drop out of treatment from the calculation of the success rate!

A set of 'standard definitions' for use in monitoring enuresis clinics and community treatment services has been published, and is available from the Bristol based Enuresis Resource and Information Centre (address at the end of this book).

Similarly, use of a declared set of practice standards and targets against which to monitor the clinic's performance is strongly recommended. These can cover issues such as the basic information and explanations to be provided to patients, frequency of patient contacts, target waiting list periods in relation to reviews of clinic capacity, and the range and availability of equipment to be maintained. Again, the Enuresis Resource and Information Centre aims to distribute suggested standards for enuresis clinics.

Progress Form

Please complete as a checklist and report on each domiciliary visit or supervision appointment
Tick boxes/fill in details as appropriate

Name of child ....

Treatment supervisor ....

Date of visit/appointment ....

Chart: Number of wet nights since last seen ....

Total number of nights since last seen ....

Tick type of alarm in use

Bed-type – twin mats ☐
Bed-type – single mat ☐
Personally worn – sound ☐
Personally worn – vibrator ☐

Is chart: Complete and up-to-date ☐ Incomplete ☐
(If incomplete; request it be kept in future)

Progress Indicators (*since last visit*)		Indications of moderate progress		Indications of good progress	
Number of wets per night:	Usually more than one	☐	Occasionally more than one	☐	No more than one per night	☐
Usual size of wet patch:	Large	☐	"Plate-sized" on sheet	☐	"Coin-sized"/wet pants only	☐
Quantity of urine to do in toilet after waking to the alarm:	None	☐	Small quantity	☐	Large quantity	☐
Waking to the alarm:	Always needs someone else to help	☐	Occasionally needs someone else to help	☐	Always wakes on own to alarm	☐
Self-waking to urinate (not woken by parent or alarm):	Never	☐	Occasionally	☐	Frequently	☐
Usual time of wetting:	Before midnight	☐	12.00 to 4.00 am	☐	After 4.00 am	☐

Progress Form (continued)

Checks to be made in bedroom (*Bed-type alarms only*)

	With two mats	With one mat		Incorrect	Correct
Alarm set up on bed in the correct sequence	Sheet Metal mat (or) [Metal mat] Sheet Metal mat [inside pillowcase] Waterproof Mattress	Sheet Mat Waterproof Mattress	Bed correctly made up?	No ☐	Yes ☐

Check alarm as made up on child's bed sounds by switching on and pressing test button or touching mats (if not, see "Problems" section below)

Alarm sounds? No ☐ Yes ☐

Sheets above and between mats should *not* be nylon (advise change if nylon being used)

Using nylon sheets? Yes ☐ No ☐

Check Procedures

(*Advise to rectify any not being followed*)

	Procedure being followed		Comment or reason if not being followed
Alarm being used every night	No ☐	Yes ☐	....
(Bed-type alarms) – child sleeps naked below the waist	No ☐	Yes ☐	....
(Personally worn alarms) Plate worn *between* two pairs of pants.	No ☐	Yes ☐	....
(Personally worn alarms) – alarm box worn and comfortably positioned on pyjama top, vest, T-shirt or wrist strap (write which), wire inside garment top	No ☐	Yes ☐	....
(Personal vibrator alarms only) – alarm box worn *inside* pyjama top/vest/T-shirt against collarbone, on wrist strap or ankle strap (write which), wire inside garment top	No ☐	Yes ☐	

Child *not parent* switches alarm off (if parent has to help child to wake, parent wakes child *before* alarm is switched off)   No ☐   Yes ☐   ....

Child visits toilet after waking to alarm   No ☐   Yes ☐   ....

Child returns to bed with dry clothing/sheets and alarm reset after wetting   No ☐   Yes ☐   ....

Parent helps child to wake *immediately* alarm sounds (unless child always wakes and can cope)   No ☐   Yes ☐   ....

Parents are avoiding waking or lifting the child to urinate unless alarm has gone off   No ☐   Yes ☐   ....

Child is allowed to drink whenever thirsty, even at bedtime   No ☐   Yes ☐   ....

Nightclothes, and ((for personally worn alarms) pants, are of non-nylon material   No ☐   Yes ☐   ....

Children not on overlearning

Has the child been totally dry for the last 14 nights?   No ☐   Yes ☐

If yes, give instructions to start overlearning (extra drinks in last hour before bed, maximum 2 pints, stop if discomfort).   *Tick to confirm if instructions to start overlearning given* ☐

Children on overlearning

Extra drinks in hour before bed: Being taken ☐   Not being taken ☐   Comment/reason if not being taken ....

Instruct to *stop* extra drinking and return to normal drinking if either: Extra drinking causes discomfort ☐   Wetting has increased to 3 or more wets in 7 ☐   Tick to confirm if you stop overlearning ☐

Progress Form (continued)

Problems (tick remedial advice taken/advised; follow sequence below)

Child does not wake to alarm	Recheck procedures	☐	Change battery	☐	Put bed alarm in tin	☐
	Change alarm type	☐	Parents to wake child with alarm each morning	☐		
'False alarms' when bed is dry	Check twin mats not touching through worn sheet or broken mesh	☐				
	Change sheets/clothing each time to remove sweat	☐				
	Reduce bedding/room temperature to reduce sweating	☐			Double sheet over bed mat	☐
	Put personally worn detector higher on pants	☐				
Alarm does not sound	Check twin mats not touching/detector or wire not broken	☐				
	Replace battery	☐	Replace alarm	☐		
Disruption from frequent wets each night	Remove alarm after first wetting	☐				
Mat(s) broken (bed-type alarm)	Replace mats	☐	(cover any break meanwhile with sticking-plaster)	☐		
Child switches bed-type alarm off without visiting toilet	Place alarm out of reach	☐				

Review

Tick if you *or either the child or his/her parent* wish treatment to be reviewed at the clinic ☐

Comments/points to watch next visit/extra procedures to be used

EIGHT

DAYTIME WETTING

Types of daytime problems

Although this book is primarily about bedwetting, families whose members bedwet are more likely than other families to come across daytime problems of urination as well. This chapter aims to give an introduction to these problems, and a brief guide to some straightforward strategies for countering them. As with bedwetting, it is important that the doctor does a medical assessment of the child with daytime wetting problems, who regularly has to empty his or her bladder extremely urgently by day, or usually needs to urinate far more frequently than other children of the same age.

Daytime pants wetting (or 'diurnal enuresis') is less common than bedwetting, affecting something between one and three per cent of all school-age children. It is often linked with bedwetting, and is an additional problem for around a quarter of all bedwetters. Daytime wetting can occur without night-time wetting and unlike bedwetting is to be found more often amongst girls than boys. The likelihood of a child growing out of daytime wetting is similar to the likelihood of bedwetting disappearing on its own as time passes – about 15 out of every 100 daytime wetters will grow out of the problem within the period of a year, without anything special being done.

Infections of the urinary system (urinary tract infections) are rather more likely in children with a daytime wetting problem, and can be one of its causes. The possibility of an infection should therefore be checked with a doctor, as should the possibility of a physical problem needing further investigation or treatment.

Urgency and frequency

Urgency and frequency in going to the toilet to urinate very commonly accompany daytime wetting. Indeed, in many cases daytime wetting is simply the result of not reaching the toilet in time, when wetting is urgent and too frequent for toilets always to be easily available. The child may get little or no warning that the bladder needs emptying, and some receive no warning at all until wetting has started to happen.

Two factors are often present in daytime wetting, and can result in urgency and frequency of the need to urinate. Firstly, the pelvic floor muscles between the child's legs may not be efficient enough to keep the bladder opening raised and so closed, with the result that there is little resistance to urine starting to flow. Secondly, the 'detrusor' muscle that makes up the walls of the bladder can be overactive, quick to produce frequent and strong contractions and so to begin squeezing urine out of the bladder. About half of all children who wet by day have this 'unstable bladder.'

One other factor is important in urgency and daytime wetting. As noted in Chapter Two, most people experience increasing urgency to 'go' as they walk towards the toilet. A moderately urgent need to urinate can become desperate as the toilet is reached. For the child (or adult) with problems in the skills of control, perhaps with an overactive bladder and an inefficient pelvic floor around its outlet as 'gatekeeper', urgency can rise so quickly and so far that wetting starts well before the toilet is reached. For some, setting out for the toilet or even thinking of going can prove too much. For others, a steep rise in urgency can cause urine to leak out just as the toilet is reached – 'going earlier' is of course not a solution to this, as it is the act of going towards the toilet, and not how full the bladder is, that is actually triggering the problem.

'Stress incontinence'

One form of daytime wetting happens when a physical stress squeezes on the bladder and forces out some urine. This leakage is called 'stress incontinence'. It can happen during coughing, sneezing, laughing or while straining the body in lifting or stretching. Quite a few children will 'leak' a little if they are tickled, and the expression 'wetting oneself with laughter' refers to this problem. Stress incontinence is common in children with other daytime bladder control difficulties, and is also common in women after childbirth (where the all-important pelvic floor has been damaged), men after a prostate operation (where the pelvic floor has been affected by the surgery) and in elderly people when the muscles of the pelvic floor are losing their tension and efficiency with age.

Figure 2 (see p. 8) showed how the outlet from the bladder is closed by the pelvic floor muscles which surround the urethra which leads from the bladder to carry urine to the outside world. Normally, when an action such as coughing or sneezing squeezes the bladder itself, the same pressure also squeezes against the urethra, just below the bladder, keeping it shut and preventing urine from being pushed through. Try a cough and you will feel this happening. If the pressure on the urethra is not enough, leakage of urine and stress incontinence will result.

'Giggle micturition'

Usually in stress incontinence, the leakage of urine stops once the physical stress (such as laughing or coughing) has stopped. Some children, particularly girls, find however that the flow of urine continues until the bladder has completely emptied. The upward tightening of the pelvic floor muscles to shut off the urine stream is just not enough to resist the powerful emptying contractions of the bladder wall (the destrusor muscle). These do not die away as they do in straightforward stress incontinence when the pelvic floor muscles manage to shut off the flow. This problem bears the impressive jargon name of 'giggle micturition' (micturition being a more fancy name for urination), because it is often triggered by laughing.

Ways of improving the situation

The following sections suggest ways in which parents and children can themselves help to reduce daytime problems in the control of urine. Whichever approach is tried, a record of progress should be kept so that the usefulness of each can be assessed, and used as the basis for a decision to abandon or continue any particular method. A reasonable trial period for any of the following would be one month. For daytime wetting, a 'wet and dry' chart (see p. 72) can be used to keep a record of wet and dry days.

These ways of helping must be agreed beforehand with your doctor, to make sure that they are appropriate in your particular case.

Holding and awareness

Practicing holding on to urine by day to reduce daytime wetting problems is not just a matter of getting the bladder used to holding more, that is, increasing its 'functional capacity'. Recent research has shown that children who wet by day do not usually have bladders that cannot cope with normal amounts of urine – daytime wetting is not particularly linked to having a limited functional bladder capacity. Not surprisingly therefore, trying to get the bladder used to holding more by simply practicing holding on to urine for longer periods by day, or 'putting off' going to the toilet for a while when the need to urinate is felt ('Retention Control Training', to be technical!), are not very helpful in treating daytime wetting. It is also important to bear in mind that if the child's bladder is unstable and squeezing hard to empty, trying to 'hold on' too much or too long can lead to a rather unhelpful 'battle' between a powerfully squeezing bladder and the pelvic floor muscles underneath it, subjecting the urinary system to a great deal of pressure in the process.

The key problem in daytime wetting is that the child is not aware enough, and does not get enough notice, of the need to empty the bladder in the toilet. It is therefore sometimes helpful to build up the ability to hold on to urine between visits to the toilet, and to notice the sensations of the bladder enough to get there in time, by starting to visit the toilet in the day very frequently and very regularly, and then only very gradually lengthening the time between visits until the child can cope with the timetable of his or her normal day (holding enough, for example, to 'last out' between break times at school).

To follow this routine, the child should visit the toilet at first each hour during the day (a small electronic timer or watch alarm will help). This needs to be started during a holiday period at home, when the timetables of being at school or away from home will not get in the way. The time between visits can then be *gradually* extended in five minute steps once the previous holding period has been managed comfortably on a number of occasions in a row. The lengthening of holding periods should be stopped when the child can cope for the minimum length of time he or she really has to last during a normal day's routine, or if a point is reached when no further progress is being made. There is no virtue in trying to go beyond the holding ability the child really needs to cope, or all one's gains may be lost again – accept that the toilet should be visited each break time at school. Holding practice should never be continued if any discomfort is felt. If at any time the child feels the urge to visit the toilet between 'scheduled' visits, he or she should go.

A further aid to increasing one's awareness of bladder sensations and the 'need to go' is to ask the child to rate his or her bladder's urgency level each time a scheduled toilet visit is due, and whenever the child feels the urge to urinate. Urgency can be rated as 'nil', 'slight', or 'urgent'. This simple 'awareness training' ploy can be tried on its own, without toileting practice, by using a timer and doing an urgency rating at hourly or two hourly intervals over a weekend.

Although simple in concept, regular toiletting and rating of awareness do require a great deal of parental supervision, and need to be carried out on days when there are not large numbers of competing activities to disrupt things. As always, it is extremely helpful to keep a record of what has been done, and what effects it has. A simple diary of practice done, coupled with a record chart showing daytime wetting at the same time, are a minimum requirement to see what is happening. A record of urgency ratings will not only help to ensure that the ratings are actually done, but also serve as a useful record of the pattern of urgency throughout the day and of any changes that may be happening in the general level of urgency. As it is often difficult to get the overall picture from words and letters on a chart, it is useful to plot key information on a graph to see clearly what is happening.

Controlling 'approach urgency'
If a child's particular problem is simply a definite, uncomfortable and severe increase in urgency to urinate as he or she approaches the toilet, perhaps wetting before reaching it, it is useful to practice controlling this 'approach urgency'. Apart from reducing the risks of wetting on the way to the toilet, a reduction in sensitivity to this form of urgency can improve overall holding ability if it is successful. The same methods can be used by adults who wish to 'tone down' the urgency involved in going to the toilet to urinate, perhaps when this is something that causes embarrassment in public or in those situations (like the middle of journeys!) when the toilet is far away but the thought of it is a nagging concern. Again, check with your doctor before trying this routine to make sure that he or she considers it appropriate for you.

Control of approach urgency can often be helped by practicing holding for increasing periods just before releasing the stream of urine into the toilet. The first step is for the child to get ready to urinate into the toilet as usual, sitting on it if a girl or standing ready at it if a boy. The child should then try to count up to ten seconds before actually 'letting go' and starting the stream. A watch with a second hand, or seconds digits, is a useful aid, but most children can learn to count the seconds (although there is a tendency to rush!). On reaching ten, urination is started. To hold on at this stage is extremely difficult for a child with urgency, but if it can be achieved with practice (and it usually can in time), it represents the significant step forward towards controlling urgency when it is at its greatest level. Progress should as usual be recorded, on a sheet on which the number of seconds of successful 'holding off' can be written at each visit to the toilet. It is often possible for this stage of control training to be practised at school as well as at home.

When the child is consistently able to count to ten at or on the toilet, the second stage is to practice counting to ten at the toilet or bathroom door as well. As this becomes odd for the person not 'in the know' to see happening, these stages need to be practised at home only.

The purpose of this routine is to weaken the hold of the approach to the toilet over the feeling of urgency. By starting the 'count to ten' routine at or on the toilet, and only going on to count at an earlier stage on the way to the toilet when the ability to 'hold off' has developed, the child is at the toilet when accidents are most likely to occur, a place where they do not matter.

Pelvic floor exercises
Figure 2 (see p. 8) illustrated the importance of the pelvic floor muscles in stopping urine from flowing from the bladder. The pelvic floor looks like a powerful wedge of muscles between the legs, through which the urethra and rectum, and in girls the vagina, pass on their way to the outside of the body. The organs of the abdomen, including the bladder, lie inside a 'basin' whose sides are largely formed by the bones of the pelvis, and whose base is formed by the pelvic floor muscles.

From the function of the pelvic floor muscles in starting, preventing and stopping urination, as described in Chapter Two, it will be realised that exercises aimed at improving the strength and control of the pelvic floor can be helpful in reducing problems such as urgency of urination or stress incontinence. However, check their suitability with your doctor first, as with all self-help treatments for daytime wetting. They may not be helpful if the bladder is very unstable.

Many mothers will be familiar with the pelvic floor exercises they were taught to use after childbirth in order to regain good bladder control. Most of these exercises can also be used by children suffering from urgency or stress incontinence, alone or linked with daytime wetting.

Two useful pelvic floor exercises for children involve practice in raising the pelvic floor and holding it 'up' for brief periods. In the first, the child should stand with legs slightly apart, or lie on his or her back with knees bent, and practise pulling the pelvic floor up into the body towards the inside of the abdomen, holding it there for a short period, and then letting it relax again. When proficient at this, he or she can practise pulling it in and up in steps, rather like a lift, pausing at each stage. He or she may start with two stages, and then see how many separate 'floors' he can make the 'lift' stop at. Pulling the pelvic floor up is like tightening yourself up to prevent diarrhoea. The child may place a hand on the pelvic floor to feel whether the movement inwards and upwards is taking place. He or she should not cheat by simply contracting the buttocks. The exercise should be repeated at least twice a day for five-minute periods.

The second exercise is to practise using the pelvic floor actually to control the stream of urine when emptying the bladder. The child should start the stream off and then practice stopping and restarting it, once on each visit to the toilet, by pulling the pelvic floor up by its own contraction and then letting it fall again to carry on urinating.

In either of these exercises, the usefulness of continuing to practice should be assessed according to progress recorded on a chart giving a rating of urgency each time the bladder is emptied, together with a record of pants wettings if the child wets by day.

Coping with smell
It is an embarrassing but familiar fact that an unpleasant smell is associated with wetting, particularly when clothing gets wet in the daytime. This often causes comment, rejection and teasing from other children. Apart from regular and thorough washing, there is one simple measure that can be taken to reduce the problem of smell. This is to dust the clothing and affected skin liberally with a powder sold by chemists under the name of 'Mycil'. Sold mainly as a treatment for athlete's foot, this preparation acts against the bacteria that are responsible for much of the stale urine smell, which can be reduced quite markedly as a result. If using this, however, do check that there is no skin reaction to it (as one should with any preparation being used regularly on the skin), and stop using it if there is.

Formal treatments

Apart from the measures already described, the professional treatment of daytime bladder control problems by doctors and others centres upon the treatment of any infection that may be present, the use of medicines, or less commonly, the use by day of a personally worn alarm. It is worth noting again here that it is quite common for daytime problems to improve to some extent if a night-time alarm is used successfully to treat bedwetting.

In a very few cases, the doctor may diagnose some other physical problem lying behind the bladder control problem, and prescribe a suitable treatment or suggest further investigations.

Treatment of infection
The parents of a child with daytime wetting, or severe urgency or frequency in emptying the bladder by day, should consult their doctor to check whether an infection is present. If so, it might be the cause of the difficulty, or, if not the cause, it may be making it worse, keeping it going, or defeating

any attempts to reduce it. Treatment of infection, usually by medication selected as likely to be effective following analysis of a urine sample, may improve bladder control problems. One should however be prepared to use other approaches as well in case it does not. Even where an infection is reducing a child's ability to control his or her bladder in the day, removal of the infection on its own does not always restore full control.

Medicines

The medicines that a doctor may prescribe to treat daytime wetting are the same as some of those likely to be used in treating night wetting. Common drugs used are Tofranil, Tryptizol, Tyrimide and Cetiprin. The drug Oxybutynin has recently been introduced in this country as a treatment for wetting problems (particularly with daytime difficulties), as a means of 'calming' an unstable bladder. Different drugs may well suit different children. As in drug treatment of bed-wetting, the aim is to reduce the responsiveness of the bladder to its contents of urine, and thus increase its 'functional capacity' and holding ability. All drug treatments for problems of bladder control seem to share a similar tendency towards relapse to wetting when the drug is stopped, whether it is stopped suddenly or gradually. It is therefore helpful to try one or more of the self-help procedures just described as well, if your doctor thinks this appropriate, in order to add an element of body-training to the chemical effects of the drug. For some children, however, medication alone does the trick permanently.

In using a drug treatment prescribed by the doctor, a record chart should be kept as with other forms of treatment, so that the need for the prescribing doctor to change the dosage or type of medicine can be considered in the light of how well the child is doing on what has been prescribed.

Daytime use of an enuresis alarm

It is possible to use a personally worn type of enuresis alarm to treat daytime wetting, if this is considered medically appropriate in a particular case. This is a rare form of treatment, since it is not practicable for the alarm to be used outside the privacy of the home, and alarm use needs to be organised for the time spent at home without visitors in the house. It is therefore limited to 'sessions' of use in the holidays, evenings and at weekends, but can be used if these sessions are likely to 'catch' enough wets for the alarm to build up a learning effect upon bladder control.

Use of a personally worn alarm by day teaches bladder control by linking the 'tightening up and stopping the stream' reaction to the sensations of a bladder that is full and beginning to contract. The alarm is triggered as soon as the detector plate, worn as described in earlier chapters but with normal outer clothing on top, becomes wet with the first of the stream of urine during an 'accident'. The sudden sound or vibration produces a jump reaction which causes the muscles of the pelvic floor to tighten up. This tends to turn the urine stream off until the toilet can be reached. On hearing the sound or feeling the vibration the child should try to hold on and make for the toilet to finish off. The alarm should be switched off as soon as is convenient, with a parent's help as needed, and then reset for next time with dry clothing. The usual record chart of wets and dries should be kept to monitor progress.

Teaching daytime control to a mentally handicapped child

Problems of bladder and bowel control are common with children who have a mental handicap, and it is often possible to improve daytime bladder control, sometimes quite markedly, by a carefully structured training programme. Such training is not as simple as it may seem, and it is wise to secure the help of someone skilled in working out and supervising training programmes with mentally handicapped children or adults. The psychologist attached to your local hospital or community service may well be in a position to advise.

The essence of such a training programme is firstly to analyse as precisely and objectively as possible the ways in which your child falls short of adequate bladder control, secondly to plan a training programme to build up the necessary skills – in small, steadily progressing steps – and thirdly, to record progress over a training period (which may be a matter of months), adapting the training programme according to its recorded results.

Analysing the problem

The basis of analysing a child's difficulties in the field of daytime bladder control is careful and detailed observation of how he or she copes with each of the fundamental skills described in Chapter Two. A concise and accurate description of what a child does can lead to a definition of what he or she needs to learn to do, and of the exact elements of the skill that he or she needs help to master. It is useful to note in a special diary exactly what a video-camera would see him or her doing – to produce a 'script' of his or her actions. It is particularly important to note events and actions in their proper sequence, and to look for common basic patterns.

An important point to bear in mind in analysing the problem is the need to allow for the possible effects of any physical handicap. It is also important to remember that while many handicapped children can be helped to improve their bladder control skills by careful training, this is not so in every case, the improvement does not necessarily reach full normal control, and much consistent, hard and painstaking work is involved.

Planning and using a training programme

Once you have identified one or more toileting skills that need developing, a training programme may be planned following straightforward learning principles. Much trial and error must be expected in finding the right combination of principles for a particular child, and to overcome the practical problems and the unexpected setbacks that often occur. Continued observation and noting of the child's actions while toileting provides the information to guide the development of the right training programme.

Rewarding desired actions is a simple but often surprisingly powerful form of training. Praise, a hug, even a sweet, can be used as an effective reward to strengthen a step in a skill which has just been achieved. It helps to 'seal in' the learning of what needs to be done. The points to follow in using a reward programme are:

1. Reward small, easily and specific 'bits' of the action being taught.
2. Be quite clear as to what the child has to do to get rewarded, and avoid the temptation to reward a 'good try' or to 'make up for' a failure (you are using the reward to seal in what has been successfully learned, not to seal in unsuccessful tries).
3. Give the reward immediately it has been earned.
4. If using sweets or food (bits of flavoured breakfast cereal are often very popular), praise the child as well. If you praise him or her just *before* giving the food reward, the effect of your praise will be strengthened by its association with the food!
5. Small rewards for small achievements are more effective than waiting for a big reward for a major achievement.
6. Record your child's progress. If there is no more progress, try a different reward; if that does not work, try breaking up the action wanted into even smaller steps to be rewarded; if that fails, rethink the strategy.
7. Give the child physical guidance in the actions to be performed, rewarding him however much guidance was needed – the guidance should then be faded out later as he or she 'picks up' on his own.
8. Once an action is well-established, begin missing out the occasional reward, then phasing the rewards out from 'every time' to 'very infrequently'. Every-time rewarding is strongest for training; occasional rewarding helps to make what has been learned a relatively permanent skill.

Three basic reward programmes are given below, with examples of how they might work out in practice:

1. Simple rewarding When a necessary piece of toileting skill does occur sometimes, but not often enough, its frequency can be increased in many cases simply by praising the child or giving a reward whenever it does happen. The rewards can be explained to a child who can understand, but will still work if the child is unable to understand what he or she is getting praised or rewarded for. (It is worth noting that the same strategy can be useful with non-handicapped children.)

An example of simple reward training is its use with a child who only very occasionally uses the toilet to urinate or defaecate, more often wetting or soiling his or her underclothing. Every time the child urinates or defaecates in the toilet, he or she is given praise, a hug and a sweet he likes, immediately he has 'performed'. The parents will record the number of toiletings each day to see whether the number is increasing, or whether the strategy needs rethinking. They will prompt and guide the child where this helps, phasing this out as he or she picks up what has to be done for himself. Once the daily frequency of successful toiletings rather than 'accidents' has reliably increased and guidance is phased out, the sweet will be left out once in every three toiletings, then left out more often, until it is rarely given and finally dropped altogether. The special praise and hug can then be reduced until toileting is 'kept going' by occasional congratulations and hugs only. (Contrary to what most people expect, use of sweets or other rewards can usually be phased out or replaced by praise alone without any difficulty – it is far rarer than one might think that a child will learn to 'do it, but only for sweets'.)

2. Shaping Often the piece of behaviour or action one wants the child to use in order to improve his or her continence never occurs, and is therefore just not there to be rewarded. 'Shaping' is a reward technique useful in such cases. The object is to mould or 'shape' the action wanted by rewarding the child (again, by praise or perhaps a small piece of something he or she likes to eat) for every move in the right direction. The principle is the same as the party game in which a person is guided towards some object or action by being told he is 'hot' or 'cold'.

A child who simply never sits on the toilet, and indeed may be rather afraid of it, can often be 'shaped' into sitting on it when asked to. At the beginning, he or she may be asked to 'go to toilet' (or whatever the usual family words are), and as soon as he or she makes the slightest move in the right direction, he is given a *small* reward. When the child moves each time, he must advance further before his reward, and so on until he must actually sit on the toilet to receive it. With one autistic boy, the author gave raisins as rewards for moves in the right direction when he was asked to go to the potty, first when the boy left his chair or where he was playing, then (standing ahead of him) halfway to the door of the room, at the door, on the landing, at the bathroom door, in the bathroom, standing by the potty, touching the potty, and finally only when he sat on the potty. Verbal instructions, gentle physical guidance, and example can be used to encourage and 'lead' the next step; the rewards effectively fuel the performance of the sequence of actions. Once it is established, the rewards for a complete shaped action can be phased out in the usual way.

3. Chaining Shaping is one way of building actions up into a complex piece of behaviour that does not occur in full on its own. 'Chaining' is a technique in which a sequence of quite separate actions can be linked together to form a complex piece of behaviour. To build a 'chain' of actions (such as removing clothing, sitting on the toilet, cleaning up, replacing clothing, flushing, and washing hands), the first step can be taught and rewarded, then instead of phasing out the reward, the next step is added so that both must be carried out, one after the other, before the reward, and so on. The secret is not to try to achieve the whole chain of events in one go, but to add the next link in the chain only when the previous ones are well-established and linked together – always rewarding the child when the latest link to be learned and added to the chain is achieved. The parent will do all the stages following this for the child. When the last in the desired chain of actions has been added, the reward for the whole sequence can be phased out gradually in the usual manner.

One can build up a chain of events by teaching and rewarding the first action first, but it is often more useful and convenient to teach the *last* link first and then build the chain backwards. An example will clarify the technique; the sequence of actions forming the chain to be learned might be those in replacing underpants and trousers after using the toilet. The links in the chain might be: stand up, hold underpants, pull up underpants, position them properly, let go, hold trousers, pull up trousers, position properly, do up zip, tuck in, do up belt. (Different children may need the sequence broken down into more or fewer steps.) To build this chain of actions *forwards*, the child is first shown how to hold his pants, rewarded when he achieves this, and then shown how to pull them up, and rewarded when he has done both in the right order – and so on until he achieves the whole sequence to receive a reward after doing up his belt. Until he reaches this point, the parent will take over after he has done his part of the chain. To build the same chain of actions *backwards*, the parent will begin by doing each stage for him up to fastening his belt, teaching him to do this last bit to finish off, and rewarding him for doing it. When he has achieved this, the next stage is added to 'his' part of the chain so that he takes over to tuck in and fasten his belt to gain his reward – and so on until he can do the whole sequence without a parent starting him off. The reward is always at the end of the chain of events, and is not phased out until the whole chain is carried out reliably. It is much more fun (and more rewarding) to be the one to finish off the successful sequence every time, than to have to hand over to someone else every time when one runs out of the bits one has learned to do for oneself!

The previous paragraphs have outlined some of the basic programmes that can be used in daytime toilet training of mentally handicapped children. The principles used are simple and fairly commonsense; the skill and effort lies in focusing straightforward training principles such as instructing and rewarding a child for small steps in the right direction, into a systematic training programme with the right strategy for the particular child involved, in one's own particular circumstances, and with a record of progress to indicate success or the need for change in a programme. The principles are few and simple, rather like the possible moves in chess, but as in chess, the combination of those rules into a successful strategy can be both challenging and difficult. There are pitfalls – it is all too easy, for example, to find that a carefully taught 'chain' becomes useless because a 'problem' link (such as the child wetting on the way to an otherwise exemplary visit to the toilet!) accidentally appears and is rewarded at the end of the chain of actions before one realises what is happening.

The purpose of mentioning such pitfalls is not to discourage parents from trying to design and carry out their own training programme, but to stress the patience and effort needed, to point out that training can often need major redesigning at various points, and that one must expect some disappointments before achieving eventual success. The effectiveness of programmes such as those described can be increased by many parents if they are able to secure the advice of someone experienced in planning and carrying out this form of training.

NINE

SOILING

This chapter is not a comprehensive guide to the problem of soiling, but is added to the chapters concerned with bedwetting and daytime problems of bladder control for the sake of completeness. The readers of a book on bedwetting in children will certainly include the parents of children who have a soiling problem as well as wetting problems, and in view of the seriousness of this problem I am adding this chapter in order to give such parents some idea of the ways of coping with it that they might pursue with the doctor.

Soiling one's underclothing with faeces (known in the jargon as 'encopresis') is one of the most humiliating problems a child can have. It is a problem that is more common amongst children with a day or night wetting problem than amongst non-wetting children; it is more common amongst boys than girls; and it is more common where there is a mental handicap. It is also a problem where there are relevant physical handicaps. Children and parents may be reassured that although soiling is more common in children who have a bedwetting or daytime wetting problem than in others, the boy or girl who has normal bowel control but wets the bed or pants will not start to soil just because he or she has poor bladder control.

Soiling is usually a daytime problem; soiling at night is very rare and certainly needs full investigation by a doctor. A medical opinion should however be sought for all children unable to control the bowel normally. As with wetting, a physical cause is rare, but needs checking for.

It is common for children with a soiling problem to be 'difficult' in varying ways, since soiling results in such a social problem for the child concerned, and is so damaging to his or her self-esteem. Many children become blasé about their problem – having little option but to develop a tough skin about it. Most have desperate strategies to try to avoid discovery when they have soiled, often hiding their soiled clothing. It is important to agree with a child who has a soiling problem an acceptable means of coping with soiled clothes – such as a covered plastic bucket of water containing a standard type of nappy-sanitiser.

Types of soiling

Retention-with-overflow

This is the most common form of soiling. It will be remembered from Chapter Two (and **Figure 3**, see p. 11) that the rectum, as the final section of the bowel, is normally an empty tube which gives rise to the sensation of needing to go to the toilet to defaecate when faeces enter it and stretch its walls. In normal bowel control, faeces enter and stretch the rectum on a more or less regular cycle, leading to defaecation (emptying the bowel, or 'passing a motion') in the toilet.

A soiling problem can arise when the child loses the signal of urgency to empty the bowel that comes from the rectum being stretched by the faeces that need emptying. This happens if faeces are regularly held for too long in the rectum instead of being emptied into the toilet, leaving it stretched for a long period. This leads to the rectum becoming adjusted to being stretched, and the stretching therefore ceases to produce the normal feelings of fullness and urgency to 'go'. The child, no longer feeling the urgency to visit the toilet, still needs to do so, however. If the bowel continues to remain unemptied, new waste material arriving in the rectum from above stretches the rectum even further and builds up a growing blockage of faeces (see **Figure 17**). If this process continues, the size of this mass can make attempts at emptying difficult and even painful – and eventually the mass of waste matter back along the large intestine can be felt from the outside, rising on the

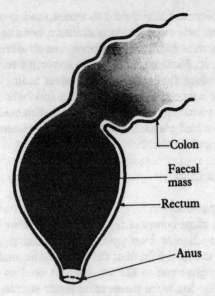

Fig.17 The rectum loaded with a faecal mass

front left side of the child's abdomen. Soiling itself begins when mainly liquid waste matter, having to go somewhere, finds its way out around the solid mass of faeces. The walls of the rectum and the circles of muscle (sphincters) which usually control any escape of faeces, being overstretched, cannot then control the inevitable leakage of liquid matter into the child's underclothes – usually without the over-stretched lower bowel even being able to inform the child that leakage is happening.

A retention-with-overflow problem can start when, over a long period, a child for some reason does not empty his or her bowel in response to feelings of urgency to 'go'. The danger signal that problems are starting is often the loss of this feeling of urgency – either by letting it pass away once it has been felt, without using the toilet (leaving the rectum stretched), or through the feelings of urgency becoming weak and infrequent. Reasons for a child not emptying the bowel despite feeling the urge to do so can be quite minor and easily overlooked. Some children tend to ignore the urge when they are engrossed in some activity, and many avoid using school toilets. It is remarkable how many school toilets have no lockable doors or toilet paper, and it is worth noting that the toilets are usually the least supervised areas of the school, and are therefore often the scene of teasing and bullying, or are occupied by those engaged in illicit activities such as smoking. Children may, quite understandably, avoid defaecation if it is painful, as it can be if there is a small split of the anus, or if the child is simply constipated. Some younger children are simply afraid of toilets, particularly strange ones away from home.

Apart from those children whose soiling problem represents a loss of previous control, there are some who have never developed a regular cycle of the rectum filling up, followed by emptying in the toilet, with the resultant risk of retention-with-overflow.

A child who might have a retention-with-overflow problem should be medically examined to establish whether there is retention. From what has been said, it will be clear that a child suspected of having this problem should not be given medicines intended to counter diarrhoea. Liquid faeces leaking into the pants may look like diarrhoea, but as the cause is a mass of hard faeces, anti-diarrhoea medication will make matters worse.

Non-control

Some children with a soiling problem do not have any retention problem, but simply do not, or have not learned to, use the toilet to empty their bowel. The bowel is emptied when the sensation of urgency arises, but in places other than the toilet. This can happen where there is a mental handicap and with a very few otherwise normal children – particularly the young child who has not yet succeeded in limiting his or her defaecation to the toilet or potty alone. The problem is really a persistence to a rather late age (say, three plus) of the accidents away from the toilet that happen in the early stages of acquiring bowel control.

It is rare, but must be stressed, that a child can have a physical problem which renders him or her unable to control the emptying of the bowel, without having any retention problem. This needs to be diagnosed through medical investigation.

Staining

The *amount* of faeces in the underclothing is important in assessing a soiling problem. Very many children (and adults) stain their underclothes with 'skid marks' quite normally, and this does not indicate anything of concern. In some cases, a child's soiling may be no more than particularly heavy staining of this type, resulting from inefficient or hurried wiping after perfectly normal defaecation.

Countermeasures to soiling

Medical examination is required in cases of severe or persistent soiling, mainly to determine whether there is a retained mass of faeces in the rectum. If so, an enema may be required to clear the retained mass. Subsequent treatment of soiling is relatively logical and straightforward, but requires persistence and meticulous routine over a period of time. The simplest retention-with-overflow cases can sometimes clear up relatively quickly, however, if the right routine is selected and strictly followed. Apart from laxatives, the concentration in treatment is more upon toileting routine than upon drugs.

As with all treatments and management procedures described in this book, a record of progress is an essential aid in confirming the usefulness of, or perhaps the need to change, the strategy being tried. A suitable record chart for the purpose is illustrated in **Figure 18**.

Regular toileting

Many children who have a problem with bowel control simply do not visit the toilet regularly to empty their bowel.

Please fill this record in every evening at bed-time. Put 'S' if the child had soiled his or her underclothes with faeces at any time during the day. Put 'C' if the child was clean throughout the day.

Name _____

Record commencing _____

	Week 1	Week 2	Week 3	Week 4	Week 5	Week 6	Week 7	Week 8	Week 9	Week 10	Week 11	Week 12
Monday												
Tuesday												
Wednesday												
Thursday												
Friday												
Saturday												
Sunday												

Fig.18 Record chart for soiling problems

The first step in trying to build up bowel control in order to solve a soiling problem is to ensure that the child does visit the toilet and try to empty his or her bowel there at a regular time at least once each day. Staying 'clean' cannot be expected without reasonably frequent use of the toilet, and a regular pattern of the rectum filling and then being emptied in the toilet is an important element in normal control. Some children with poor bowel control can be helped, surprisingly perhaps, by doing nothing more complicated than ensuring that they go to the toilet once a day regularly, and again whenever they feel the urge to go (this is important to avoid the rectum being left stretched with faeces for long periods).

*Intensive toileting**

Where a child has developed a severe retention-with-overflow problem, and may have lost the vital urgency signal through continuous stretching of the rectum, a more intensive toileting routine will probably be needed. Medical opinion should be sought first, as the initial step in resolving the problem may well be an enema to remove the mass of faeces that has built up in the rectum.

The object, once any serious retention is removed, is to keep the rectum empty – to avoid any further build-up of retained faeces, and to allow the walls of the rectum to regain their sensitivity to being stretched (and giving the sensation of the 'need to go') by the arrival of new faeces in the rectum. Intensive toileting is simple, but *must* be carried out strictly and consistently. It involves three elements:

1. A mild laxative taken last thing at night. Check with your doctor first that this is suitable for your child, and follow his or her recommendation on the type of laxative to use. Some doctors may prescribe suppositories rather than a mild laxative for the same purpose, to achieve a greater and more direct effect. The laxative will make

* This treatment technique was developed by my former colleague, Dr Gordon Young.

the child more likely to defaecate in the morning, and will ensure that the faeces are soft and easy to pass into the toilet, and not likely to start 'setting' again into a retained mass.

2. A warm drink after breakfast every morning. It is its warmth, rather than what it is, that matters. The warm drink serves to set in motion the waves of muscular contractions ('peristalsis') along the tubing of the gut, that help to push the faeces out from the rectum.

3. Twenty minutes after the warm drink, the child should visit the toilet and try to empty his or her bowel. This is generally the time taken for the muscular contractions set off by the drink to reach the rectum. With both the laxative and the warm drink, the child will now be visiting the toilet at a time when defaecation is most likely to happen.

This intensive toileting routine should be kept going until soiling has stopped for at least two weeks. One should allow up to three months for this to occur, although in some cases a quite rapid response can occur. The treatment is successful for a proportion, but certainly not all, cases of retention-with-overflow soiling in children. The research is limited, but from experience the chances of success in a given case can be estimated as in the region of fifty-fifty.

Once two weeks free of soiling have been achieved, the laxative may be discontinued, but the regular toileting pattern should be continued permanently. It is helpful if the warm drink is continued as well. If the progress record shows little improvement after a few weeks, the warm drink, 20-minute wait and toileting, can be repeated after each meal as well as after breakfast.

Many parents are surprised at first when laxatives are suggested for children who soil – it does seem at first sight to fly in the face of logic! The reason can be appreciated when it is known that a particular child has a retention problem behind his or her soiling. As has been noted, what might seem logical

– to give the child anti-diarrhoea medicine – must be avoided as it will simply aggravate the problem.

Reacting to urgency

From Chapter Two it may be recalled that although the bladder is normally partially full, the rectum should normally be kept empty. To prevent the build-up of a retained mass of faeces, with the risk of losing the vital stretch-urgency signal, a child who feels urgency to empty his or her bowel should always take notice of this and visit a toilet as soon as possible. By doing this he or she will avoid leaving the rectum stretched and full for more than short periods, thus ensuring that he will continue to receive the urgency signal whenever faeces pass into the rectum and need emptying. Regular or intensive toilet training will encourage this to happen, and also encourage it to happen at roughly the same time or times each day to establish a regular pattern of filling and emptying.

The golden rule for the child is: *when you have the urge to empty your bowel, use the toilet before the urge has time to pass away*. If the child does let the urge pass away, he or she should still visit the toilet as soon as possible afterwards – not just leave it. Explain that the urge does not disappear because he or she no longer needs to go, but because his or her rectum is becoming dangerously used to being stretched. The faeces have not disappeared, but are still there to be emptied.

Diet

It is worth reviewing the diet of any child with a soiling problem. A poor diet is unlikely to be the cause of severe soiling, but it can adversely affect bowel regularity and the consistency of the faeces enough to put whatever bowel control there is under severe strain, and to stop progress towards solving the soiling. A diet tending to lead to 'loose' faeces can cause problems where regular toileting is not regularly established and there is a degree of 'non-control'. One leading towards constipation can make defaecation difficult and encourage retention. Many children consume a fascinating diet, with firm likes and dislikes and more 'convenience' foods and foods of one particular type or another, than is appropriate. If the child's usual diet is short on roughage and variety, it is worth adjusting it.

Changes in a child's diet need to be based on explanation to the child of the reasons for the change, and (as far as is possible) agreement over the changes to be made. Parental experience shows that 'because it's better for you' does not always achieve the desired results! 'Healthy eating' may not be the most popular diet, but is now more socially acceptable than it has ever been.

The most appropriate diet to help reduce the risks of soiling will contain a reasonable amount of 'roughage' (fibre), to make the faeces more likely to be bulky but soft and easy both to pass and control. Foods likely to achieve this include wholegrain breakfast cereals (of which there is a wide variety available, with plenty of information on the boxes about the fibre they contain), porridge, wholemeal bread or toast, and fruit (rather than sweets!). What children see as being an 'ordinary dinner' is good for the purpose, with meat or fish, potatoes and green or root vegetables; so is salad. The child should drink a reasonable amount during the day – the liquid is necessary with the fibre to get the consistency of the faeces right.

One should however avoid too sudden a change in a child's diet: the body does need time to adjust to major changes, otherwise other problems (like wind) can be produced. It is important to note that one is trying to achieve a balanced diet with a normal proportion of fibre in it if it is short on roughage to start with. This does not mean that the 'fun' aspects of a child's diet, like the sweets, cakes and fried food, have to be cut out – only that they have to be kept in proportion.

Reward training

In 'non-control' cases, particularly with a mentally handicapped child or young person, the reward-training principle described in the last chapter can be used to help train the child to use the toilet as is necessary to stay clean. With a non-control problem, with both normal and mentally handicapped children, it is helpful to give praise and rewards for two things. Firstly, for producing faeces in the toilet, and secondly for periods of keeping the pants clean (the child can be 'checked' at intervals).

The use of rewards is helpful with many children with poor bowel control, but needs adapting according to the particular child. The mentally handicapped or quite young child can be checked and closely supervised, and can be rewarded immediately – either with something to eat, or with points that can be saved up (rather like cash) towards some treat or reward. With an older child, points or even coins (not too high a value!) can be used, and for many, working out and keeping up their own records of progress can be rewarding. A simple record, without any rewards as such to back it up, can sometimes have the same effect as a basic reward system in reinforcing and encouraging the learning of control skills.

Accepting the toilet

An important factor in the relief of soiling for many children is encouragement to use the toilet when necessary away from home, especially at school. The problems of school toilets without privacy or paper have already been mentioned; these can put off a child from using the toilet at school sufficiently to cause bowel control problems. It is easy to be put off by 'adverse toilets', as many adults will realise if they have ever encountered abroad the type of toilet which requires one to straddle a hole in the floor.

Children can be helped to use school toilets by very simple strategies, depending upon their particular worry. A pad of toilet paper can be carried from home, an arrangement can be reached with the teacher for the child to visit the toilet during class, when other children are not there, or a trusted friend may 'stand guard' outside the door. The soiling problem at school of one patient of mine was resolved when he was equipped with a steel ruler to hold the school toilet door closed.

A very small number of children are actually afraid of

sitting on the toilet. The most useful solution to try for this rare but possible problem is to take the child towards the toilet, and eventually to sit on it, *gradually*, in small steps, and only as the child feels able to cope with each step. One should start at a distance at which the child is happy, and simply 'introduce' him a little closer (and for a little longer) at each attempt. Praise and specific rewards can help in addition to this 'gradual introduction' approach.

FURTHER READING

Azrin, N. and Foxx, R., *Toilet Training in Less than a Day*, London, Macmillan, 1975. An intensive toilet training programme.

Hamilton, B., *Urinary and faecal incontinence*, Mitcham, Age Concern England, 1987. A series of ten brief leaflets on incontinence in elderly people.

Kolvin, I., MacKeith, R. C. and Meadow, R. S. (Eds), *Bladder Control and Enuresis*, London, Heinemann Medical, 1973. Collected research reports and major reviews on many aspects of enuresis.

Mandelstam, D., *Incontinence and its Management*, London, Croom Helm, 1980. A valuable handbook on the problems of incontinence in adults.

Montgomery, E., *Regaining bladder control*, Bristol, Wright, 1974. Contains useful pelvic floor exercises.

ADDRESSES

Enuresis Resource and Information Centre
65 St Michaels Hill, Bristol B52 8DZ.
Provides an advisory service and literature on enuresis for parents, families and professionals.

The Enuresis Treatment Service
38 Woodstock Road East, Begbroke, Oxford OX5 7RG.
The author's treatment service; a registered charity which offers the 'Treatline' service for treatment by regular postal and telephone contact.

APPENDIX

DEPARTMENT OF HEALTH
AND SOCIAL SECURITY

ENURESIS ALARMS AND CONTINENCE TRAINING DEVICES

A Revised Performance Specification
(R/E 1004/03 ISSUE II)

BASIC SAFETY REQUIREMENTS

1. The equipment shall comply with BS5724 Part 1, except where the requirements of BS5724 are varied by the following.

2. Except for currents above 100Hz, the maximum current that the detection electrodes can draw from the alarm shall not exceed 10 microamperes where the patient is normally in contact with both electrodes, or 100 microamperes where the patient is normally in contact with only one electrode. The current may be dc, ac, hf or pulsatile. For currents other than dc the values shall refer to the rms current. For currents above 100Hz the allowable current may be increased according to the inverse of the curve given in BS5724 Fig. 15 (1979 Edition), but subject to a maximum current at any frequency of ten times the values given above.

3. Where the detection electrodes use the principle of electrolytic generation of current, the above limits shall be observed, and the electrode arrangement shall be such that the patient is normally in contact with only one electrode.

4. Potentials exceeding 15 volts shall not be used or generated in the circuit. This requirement includes transient voltages which may be produced by inductive components.

5. Exposed metal parts of the alarm shall be electrically isolated from the detection electrodes.

6. The wires from the alarm should be attached permanently to the detection electrodes or be connected to them in such a way that unintentional disconnection is not likely.

7. The equipment shall be battery powered.

8. Plug connectors which fit standard mains sockets shall not be used.

9. Mains colour coded wire (blue and brown) shall not be used for any external connections.

10. Connections to the alarm for different purposes, e.g. extension alarms and detection electrodes shall not be interchangeable.

Operating Requirements:

1. Once triggered, the alarm shall continue to operate until reset by a switch.

2. Either a summary of the instructions for use shall be printed on the alarm, or if there is insufficient space, the user's attention shall be drawn to the instructions for use by a suitable indication on the equipment.

Recommended Facility:

1. For equipment intended for use with sleeping patients, a low power visual indication should be provided which lights when the audible alarm sounds. This provides reassurance to the patient when woken, and enables the controls to be seen.

Possible Facilities:

1. A socket into which an extension alarm may be plugged.

2. A switch to cut out the audible alarm to leave only the visual indication.
   (*Reproduced by permission*)

ALEX GRIFFITHS and
DOROTHY HAMILTON

LEARNING AT HOME

This book will help all parents
to help their children

Parents already contribute much to their children's learning, and with comparatively little effort can do much more.

It is now firmly established that where parents and teachers co-operate over children's education, the effects on learning are remarkable. This practical handbook describes how you can co-operate with your child's teachers to help your child with reading, writing, mathematics and other curriculum areas. What matters is the approach to learning, rather than specific knowledge: enjoyment, interest and fun are the keynotes for success.

ANNE N. WALTHER

DIVORCE HANGOVER

A prescription for a
brighter future

Divorce is devastating. It ranks as the most serious life crisis after the death of a spouse. Intense feelings of loss, anger, guilt and loneliness are its normal and natural consequences. But if they take over and prevent you from coping with daily life, then you have a divorce hangover.

This practical and carefully constructed guide will help you recognise and accept the changes that divorce inevitably brings. Step by step it will free you of self-destructive emotions, encourage you to rediscover personal strengths and enable you to develop constructive strategies for relating to your ex-spouse, children, friends, family – and a new mate. Above all, it will convince you that *you* are your own best asset.

DR. CHARLES SHEPHERD

LIVING WITH M.E.

It is estimated that there are over 100,000 people suffering from M.E. in Britain today. M.E. is short for *myalgic encephalomyelitis*, a term which relates to the parts of the body affected: *myalgic*, the muscles; *encephalo*, the brain; and *myelitis*, the nerves. The principal symptoms are intense muscle fatigue and brain malfunction following a flu-like infection.

Until recently, many people suffering from M.E. had great difficulty in finding a diagnosis and a way of dealing effectively with the disease. This guide provides much-needed basic information about M.E. The symptoms are described in detail and there is also information on the viruses thought to be responsible for M.E., what triggers it and who can get it. Additional problems, such as disordered sleep, depression, pain in the joints and difficulties with the eyes, ears and balance are also discussed.

'A well-researched, up-to-date guide written from an orthodox medical viewpoint . . . the one to buy for any sufferer who wants information based on science, not speculation.'
M.E. Action Campaign Newsletter

JANE R. HIRSCHMANN
and CAROL H. MUNTER

OVERCOMING OVEREATING

Conquer your obsession with food

Lose weight naturally

Enjoy the food you most desire

**Forget your preoccupation with eating
and weight**

Discover the freedom of no restraints

Give up dieting forever

Overcoming Overeating **makes this all possible, for the authors have returned eating to its natural place in life, so that food becomes something to be enjoyed rather than feared.**

  Concentrating on the normal physiological hunger that we all experience, Jane R. Hirschmann and Carol H. Munter help you to break out of the lonely cycle of diet, binge, recrimination and self-loathing. Both practical and reassuring, they offer radical, realistic guidance on how to conquer an obsession and restore the compulsive eater's self-esteem.

'*Overcoming Overeating* will stand out from the
crowd of diet books for its caring response to the
compulsive eater.'
Susie Orbach, author of *Fat is a Feminist Issue*

A Full List of Cedar Books

While every effort is made to keep prices low, it is sometimes necessary to increase prices at short notice. Mandarin Paperbacks reserves the right to show new retail prices on covers which may differ from those previously advertised in the text or elsewhere.

The prices shown below were correct at the time of going to press.

☐	7493 0791 9	**New Arthritis and Common Sense:**	
		A Complete Guide to Effective Relief	Dale Alexander £4.99
☐	7493 0046 9	**Sex and Your Health**	James Bevan £4.99
☐	7493 0938 5	**The Courage to Heal**	Ellen Bass and Laura Davis £7.99
☐	7493 0856 7	**The Body Has Its Reasons: Anti Exercises**	
		and Self-awareness	Therese Bertherat and Carol Bernstein £4.99
☐	434 11137 6	**I Only Want What's Best For You**	Judith Brown £3.95
☐	7493 0579 7	**How to Develop Self-Confidence and Influence**	
		People by Public Speaking	Dale Carnegie £4.99
☐	7493 0593 2	**How to Enjoy Your Life and Your Job**	Dale Carnegie £4.99
☐	7493 0723 4	**How to Stop Worrying and Start Living**	Dale Carnegie £4.99
☐	7493 0784 6	**How to Win Friends and Influence People**	Dale Carnegie £4.99
☐	7493 0577 0	**The Quick and Easy Way to Effective Speaking**	Dale Carnegie £4.99
☐	7493 0098 1	**Divorced Parenting**	Dr Sol Goldstein £4.50
☐	7493 1047 2	**Learning at Home**	Griffiths and Hamilton £4.99
☐	7493 0740 4	**New Parents**	David Harvey £6.99
☐	7493 1033 2	**Carbohydrate Addict's Diet**	Dr Rachael Heller and Dr Richard Heller £4.99
☐	7493 0246 1	**Overcoming Overeating**	Jane Hirschmann & Carol Munter £3.99
☐	7493 0322 0	**Women, Sex and Addiction**	Charlotte Davis Kasl £4.99
☐	7493 0713 7	**Living Together Feeling Alone**	Dr Dan Kiley £4.99
☐	434 11121 X	**C-Zone: Peak Performance Under Pressure**	Robert Kriegel and
			Marilyn Kriegel £3.95
☐	7493 0090 6	**Helping Your Anxious Child**	David Lewis £4.99
☐	7493 1340 4	**The Treatment Handbook for 300 Common**	
		Ailments	Dr Roy McGregor £7.95
☐	7493 1079 0	**Help For the Bed-Wetting Child**	Dr Roger Morgan £4.99
☐	7493 1019 7	**How to be Your Own Best Friend**	Mildred Newman and Bernard Berkowitz £4.99
☐	7493 0933 4	**The Amazing Results of Positive Thinking**	Norman Vincent Peale £4.99
☐	434 11167 8	**Courage and Confidence**	Norman Vincent Peale £4.99
☐	7493 0880 X	**Enthusiasm Makes The Difference**	Norman Vincent Peale £4.99
☐	7493 0569 X	**A Guide to Confident Living**	Norman Vincent Peale £4.99
☐	7493 0719 6	**Inspiring Messages for Daily Living**	Norman Vincent Peale £4.99
☐	7493 0716 1	**Joy and Enthusiasm**	Norman Vincent Peale £4.99
☐	7493 1220 3	**The New Art of Living**	Norman Vincent Peale £3.95
☐	7493 0720 X	**Positive Thoughts For The Day**	Norman Vincent Peale £4.99
☐	7493 0858 3	**The Positive Way to Change Your Life**	Norman Vincent Peale £4.99
☐	7493 0821 4	**The Power of Positive Living**	Norman Vincent Peale £4.99
☐	7493 0715 3	**The Power of Positive Thinking**	Norman Vincent Peale £4.99
☐	7493 0567 3	**The Power of Positive Thinking for Young**	
		People	Norman Vincent Peale £4.99
☐	7493 1023 5	**The Power of the Plus Factor**	Norman Vincent Peale £4.99
☐	7493 0881 8	**The Tough Minded Optimist**	Norman Vincent Peale £4.99
☐	7493 0254 2	**Families and How to Survive Them**	Robin Skynner and John Cleese £5.99
☐	7493 1041 0	**How to Survive in Spite of Your Parents**	Dr Margaret Reinhold £5.99
☐	7493 1018 9	**When Am I Going to be Happy**	Dr Penelope Russianoff £5.99
☐	7493 0733 1	**When You and Your Mother Can't be Friends**	Victoria Secunda £5.99
☐	7493 0724 2	**Living with ME: A Self Help Guide**	Dr Charles Shepherd £4.99